# The Essence of a Single-Session Success

# Ericksonian Monographs

Ericksonian Monographs　　　Number 9

# The Essence of a Single-Session Success

### Edited by
### Stephen R. Lankton, M.S.W.
### Kristina K. Erickson, M.S., M.D.

# Brunner/Mazel Publishers • New York

Library of Congress Cataloging-in-Publication Data

The Essence of a single-session success / edited by Stephen R. Lankton
and Kristina K. Erickson.
    p.    cm. — (Ericksonian monographs : no. 9)
    Includes bibliographical references.
    ISBN 0-87630-727-6
    1. Single-session psychotherapy—Case studies.  2. Hypnotism—
Therapeutic use—Case studies.  3. Single-session psychotherapy.
4. Hypnotism—Therapeutic use. 5. Erickson, Milton H.   I. Lankton,
Stephen R.   II. Erickson, Kristina K.   III. Series.
RC480.55.E88     1994
616.89′14—dc20                                                    93-11832
                                                                          CIP

*Published by*
BRUNNER/MAZEL, INC.
19 Union Square West
New York, New York 10003

MANUFACTURED IN THE UNITED STATES OF AMERICA

10 9 8 7 6 5 4 3 2 1

# Ericksonian Monographs

The *Ericksonian Monographs* publish only original manuscripts dealing with Ericksonian approaches to hypnosis, family therapy, and psychotherapy, including techniques, case studies, research, and theory.

The *Monographs* will publish only those articles of highest quality that foster the growth and development of the Ericksonian approach and exemplify an original contribution to the fields of physical and mental health. In keeping with the purpose of the *Monographs*, articles should be prepared so that they are readable by a heterogeneous audience of professionals in psychology, medicine, social work, dentistry, and related clinical fields.

Publication of the *Ericksonian Monographs* shall be on an irregular basis, no more than three times per year. The *Monographs* are a numbered, periodical publication. Dates of publication are determined by the quantity of high-quality articles accepted by the Editorial Board and the Board of Directors of the Milton H. Erickson Foundation, Inc., rather than by calendar dates.

## Advice for Authors

**Manuscripts** should be *submitted in quintuplicate* (five copies) with a 100–150-word abstract to Stephen R. Lankton, M.S.W., P.O. Box 958, Gulf Breeze, FL 32562-0958. Manuscripts of lengths varying from 15 to 100 typed double-spaced pages will be considered for publication. Submitted manuscripts cannot be returned to authors. Authors using electronic storage should also send a floppy disk containing the file. Authors with telecommunications capability may pre-submit one copy electronically in ASCII, Word, WFW, or WP (or other) format at any baud rate up to 57,600 bps and with the following communication parameters: 8-bit word size, no parity, one stop bit; several transfer protocols are available. FAX submission is also available. FAX calls are received 24 hours per day at 904-932-3118. Call 904-932-6819 (voice) for any additional help.

**Style and format** of submitted manuscripts must adhere to the instructions described in the *Publication Manual of the American Psychological Association* (third edition, 1983). The manuscripts will be returned for revision if reference citations, preparation of tables and figures, manuscript format, avoidance of sexist language, copyright permission for cited material, title-page style, etc., do not conform to the *Manual*.

**Copyright** ownership must be transferred to the Milton H. Erickson Foundation, Inc., if your manuscript is accepted for publication. The Editor's acceptance letter will include a form explaining copyright release, ownership, and privileges.

**Reference citations** should be scrutinized with special care to credit originality and avoid plagiarism. Referenced material should be carefully checked by the author prior to the first submission of the manuscript.

**Charts and photographs** accompanying the manuscripts must be presented in camera-ready form.

**Copy editing and galley proofs** will be sent to the authors for revisions. Manuscripts must be submitted in clearly written, acceptable, scholarly English. Neither the Editor nor the Publisher is responsible for correcting errors of spelling and grammar: the manuscript, after acceptance, should be immediately ready for publication. Authors should understand that a charge will be passed on to them by the publisher for revision of galleys.

**Indexing** will be done with both a name and a key-word reference. When you submit your paper, include a list of key words and key concepts. These will be put into the computer prior to typesetting, and will be used to generate an index. Please understand that the terms selected will be referenced across all papers; therefore, be judicious about your choices. Also, supply a list of all names that you want to appear in the name index. Please do not include Dr. Erickson's name. It would be too unwieldy to reference him in the entire text.

**Prescreening and review procedures** for articles are outlined below. Priority is given to those articles that conform to the designated theme for the upcoming *Monographs*. All manuscripts will be prescreened, without the author's name, by the Editor or one member of the Editorial Board and one member of either the Continuing Medical Education (CME) Committee or the Board of Directors of the Milton H. Erickson Foundation, Inc.

**Final acceptance** of all articles is at the discretion of the Board of Directors of the Milton H. Erickson Foundation, Inc. Their decisions will be made after acceptable prescreened articles have been reviewed and edited by a minimum of four persons: two Editorial Board members, one member of the CME committee or the Board of Directors, and the Editor. Occasionally, reviewers selected by the Editor will assist in compiling feedback to authors. The final copy of an accepted paper should be sent also on a floppy disk by authors using electronic storage.

**Feedback for authors and manuscript revision** will be handled by the Editor between one and two months after submission of the prepared manuscript. Additional inquiries are welcome if addressed to the Editor.

# Contents

# Contributors

**Janet Sasson Edgette, Psy.D.** Milton H. Erickson Institute, Philadelphia, PA

**Gregg Eichenfield, Ph.D.** Associate Professor, Department of Professional Psychology, University of Saint Thomas, St. Paul, MN

**Kristina K. Erickson, M.S., M.D.** Board of Directors, Milton H. Erickson Foundation, Inc., Phoenix, AZ; Emergency Medicine, N.W. Hospital, Tucson, AZ

**Betty Alice Erickson, M.S., L.P.C.** private practice, Dallas, TX

**Jeffrey B. Feldman, Ph.D.** Charlotte Institute of Rehabilitation, Charlotte, NC

**Richard Fisch, M.D.** Clinical Associate Professor of Psychiatry, Stanford, CA; Director, Brief Therapy Center, Mental Research Institute, Palo Alto, CA

**Jay Haley** Director, Family Therapy Institute, Rockwell, MD

**Lynn D. Johnson, Ph.D.** Brief Therapy Center, Salt Lake City, UT

**Bradford P. Keeney, Ph.D.** Professor, Department of Professional Psychology, University of Saint Thomas, St. Paul, MN

**Carol J. Kershaw, Ed.D.** Codirector, Milton H. Erickson Institute, Houston, TX

**Stephen R. Lankton, M.S.W., D.A.H.B.** Department of Psychology, University of West Florida; private practice, Gulf Breeze, FL

**William J. Matthews, Ph.D.** Associate Professor, Counseling Psychology, University of Massachusetts, Amherst, MA

**Akira Otani, Ed.D.** University of Maryland Counseling Center, College Park, MD

**Jane Parsons-Fein, CSWBCD,** Director of Training, New York Society for Ericksonian Psychotherapy and Hypnosis

**Robert Pearson, M.D.** private practice, Houston, TX

**Robert Schwarz, Psy.D.** Director, Institute for Advanced Training, Philadelphia, PA

# Introduction

I am most pleased to present the current volume of the *Ericksonian Monographs*. I have given it the title "The Essence of a Single-Session Success." The reason for this will be apparent, as the majority of the issue concerns the commentary from nine experts responding to a successful single brief therapy session. This session concerned a client suffering from chronic anxiety and severe anxiety attacks. In addition, this *Monograph* includes four superb articles that provide thoughtful material in the areas of theory, context, case research, and short-term therapy, as well as a look at Milton Erickson's explanation of his own work!

Jay Haley, who is regarded as one of the foremost experts on Milton Erickson's work, transcribed a 30-year-old kinescope film of M. H. Erickson's work. Haley studied this film, met with Dr. Erickson in 1972, and together they viewed and discussed the film. This presentation provides an informative glimpse into Erickson's own analysis of his work, punctuated, probed, and questioned by Jay Haley.

Akira Otani, Ph.D., from the University of Maryland Counseling Center, who provided several excellent research articles in past volumes, has taken a long-overdue look at the importance of "context" in Ericksonian therapy. Otani examined 29 Ericksonian interventions and explained them as contextual change maneuvers classified into six major types. An important contribution in this article is the clarity with which Otani illustrates the fundamental importance of considering the presence of contextual framing in the process of growth and change.

Jeffrey Feldman, Ph.D., has contributed an article describing a theoretical framework he has called "A Multischema Model for Combining Ericksonian and Cognitive Therapy." In this article, he unites cognitive therapy frameworks so as to apply both conscious and unconscious attitudes. He then shows practical applications of the concept and framework with two cases employing Ericksonian techniques.

In "Electron Theory and the Single-Session Therapy," Janet Sasson Edgette, Psy.D., illustrates two cases in which she succeeds by means of a single-session intervention. This is perhaps best characterized as utilizing the unconscious conflict without trying to change it. She provides a thoughtful discussion of this truncated therapy.

All remaining articles refer to a complete transcript of a single brief therapy session. Some time ago, I asked Stephen Lankton, M.S.W., to furnish a transcript from his practice of a single, complete, session of therapy with a successful outcome. The proposal was to send the transcript to renowned and diverse experts, soliciting their reviews and comments, and, in particular, their opinions as to why this session was a success. An audio- and videotape and a written transcript (which is included in this issue) were sent to Richard Fisch, M.D., William Matthews, Ph.D., Lynn Johnson, Ph.D., Robert Schwarz, Psy.D., Jane Parsons-Fein, M.S.W., Bradford P. Keeney, Ph.D., Gregg Eichenfield, Ph.D., Carol Kershaw, Ed.D., Betty Erickson-Elliott, M.S., L.P.C., and Robert Pearson, M.D. This talented group then submitted their analyses and comments to the *Monographs*.

I anticipated a wide and stimulating diversity of opinions and discussions covering a broad spectrum of concepts and interpretations. What I received was all of that, and a rich array of inspiring thought and commentary about how therapy can be interpreted and viewed. The range of opinions and discussion offers stimulating educational material. This is particularly helpful as one is able to refer to the commonality of the single-case transcript as one studies and reflects on the different comments and insights.

An associate professor at the University of Massachusetts, William Matthews, Ph.D., has commented in a detailed manner, referring to incidents of seeding, movement, rapport, and experience retrieval and organization. While juggling this detailed account of events, he never loses sight of the overall organization of the therapy, and by so doing teaches a great deal about the orchestration of the therapeutic conversation.

In his "Commentary on a Therapy with Joan," Robert Schwarz, Psy.D., presents a well-documented array of interventions seen from a state-of-consciousness model. This involved finding and perturbing the client's negative presuppositions, addressing her problem at varying levels, and using mutually reinforcing suggestions, which allowed her to weave together a more useful state of consciousness to help her meet her current life demands.

Senior research director at the Mental Research Institute, Richard Fisch, M.D., offers us an invaluable set of lessons in his response, "Case Commentary: A Woman with Chronic Anxiety and Panic Attacks." He tells us that the initial key element is the one-down, "just being human" approach taken by a therapist. Following this, an important factor is the continual setting of an implicit expectation of improvement. Other factors are normalizing pathology, such as by implicitly challenging presuppositions, expressing ideas in an evocative manner, and repetition.

Bradford P. Keeney, Ph.D., and Gregg Eichenfield, Ph.D., asked 30 therapists with diverse backgrounds to respond to what they called "transformational moments" in the therapy session, and found a remarkable similarity among the responses. They discuss these moments, and give us a better understanding of what they mean by the "dramaturgical essence of therapy."

An article called "Trickster Coyote Meets the February Mother: A Commentary on Lankton's Case Transcript" by Lynn D. Johnson, Ph.D., shows once again that irrepressible talent that Dr. Johnson has for seeing events from a unique and useful angle. His observation of the therapist as presenting an increasingly poignant and organized presentation therapy that may be most effective when its start is purposefully casual and faltering is ingenious.

Carol Kershaw, Ed.D., saw the session as a mutual rewrite of the client's story. As Kershaw saw it, the therapist used the context of story to provide guidance and a parental mode that allowed for a nurturing self-worth, self-esteem, and an enjoyment of living in this client.

In the "Comment on Therapy by Stephen Lankton, M.S.W.: Case of a Woman with Chronic Anxiety and Panic Attacks," Betty Erickson, M.S., L.P.C., shows her skill by articulating some subtle connections so well that they come alive and underscore how she views critical incidents in therapy. Erickson makes similarly well-conceived and expressed comments on the usefulness of humor in therapy.

Robert Pearson, M.D., a long-time associate of Dr. Erickson's, is true to form with a "down-to-earth" summary of therapeutic ingredients. Pearson describes four factors that converge to engage this client: a desire for change, demand characteristics, a critical moment of reframing, and therapeutic emphasis placed on the use of strengths.

Jane Parsons-Fein, M.S.W., presents an eloquent collage of ideas suggesting that the success in this case resulted from a series of creative moments. She contends that these moments touched the client's sensory motoric system, and uses the transcript to trace both the process and content that contributed to this impact.

Thus I present the ninth *Ericksonian Monographs* — a complex assortment of stimulating articles that will present our readers with food for thought. In reading this issue, we remind the reader that single-session therapy is appropriate, or even possible, in only certain select instances. By providing an example of such therapy here, we hope we have given the reader a better understanding of what is germane to these cases when they occur. With the inclusion of the other four stimulating articles, this issue brings a well-rounded, dynamic collection of thoughtful and provocative material to the reader's desk.

*Kristina K. Erickson, M.S., M.D.*

# The Essence of a Single-Session Success

# Erickson Hypnotic Demonstration: 1964*

## Jay Haley

*This is a presentation of the text of an hypnotic demonstration by Milton H. Erickson, M.D., in 1964. At a medical meeting he hypnotized a series of volunteer subjects, and it is one of the few demonstrations of this type which was filmed. In 1972 Erickson was shown the film and asked to comment on why he did what he did in the hypnotic inductions. This paper presents the full transcript of the demonstration, along with Erickson's comments upon it, and my own discussion of it. The emphasis is upon hypnosis from the communication point of view.*

Over the years, Milton H. Erickson, M.D., conducted many hypnotic demonstrations at seminars and medical meetings. Occasional audiotapes were made of these demonstrations, but he was rarely filmed in those early years when he was in his prime. There was no videotape available at that time, and 16 mm film was expensive. Without film, there was no opportunity to carefully analyze the visual as well as the audio presentation of his hypnotic work.

In 1964, at a meeting of the American Society for Clinical Hypnosis in Philadelphia, Erickson did an hypnotic demonstration for a medical audience. It was apparently kinescoped, the process prior to videotape, and later that was turned into an edited 16mm film, which was technically poor in sound and picture, with parts cut out. Erickson gave me the copy of the film, and for a number of years I used it to teach his approach to hypnosis. Because of many questions I had about what he did in that demonstration, I took the film to Phoenix in 1972 and showed it to him, asking him to explain why he did what he did during the demonstration.

My own interest has been in understanding the hypnotic process in

*This chapter also appears in *Jay Haley on Milton H. Erickson*, by Jay Haley. New York: Brunner/Mazel, Inc., 1993.

Address correspondence to Jay Haley, Family Therapy Institute, 5850 Hubbard Drive, Rockville, MD 20852.

1

terms of communication, and this film provides the opportunity to both see and hear what Dr. Erickson said and how the subject responded. For example, when he tells a subject to awaken and the subject is puzzled as to why her hand stays up in the air, I am puzzled as well. It requires careful study of the film to develop an hypothesis about just what Erickson said when he appeared to awaken her but did not awaken her. Obviously, the hypnotic communication interchange is a complex and intricate one that is worth examining again and again when it is on film.

In this presentation, I will offer the text of the film and my later conversation with Erickson about it. I will also add my own comments about what I believe he was saying and doing. It might seem presumptuous of me to offer my own explanation, particularly when it differs from that of Erickson, but I think it is justified. At the time of this discussion, it had been 20 years since I attended my first seminar with Erickson, and I had spent hundreds of hours talking with him about hypnosis and therapy as part of my research. Therefore, I was familiar with many of his ideas. I have also done many research interviews with therapists, and I often found that what they considered themselves to be doing could be seen in a quite different perspective by an outsider who is examining the interview.

Another reason for adding my own comments is that Erickson's memory of this demonstration was limited because he had been ill at the time. As the discussion progressed, he seemed to remember more about it. The reader here can keep the opinions separate since I present them in different typestyles. In my comments, I might point out some things that seem elementary to an experienced hypnotist, but I think it helps most readers to understand what is happening. In his comments on this film, Erickson is not talking at an elementary level. This text also provides an historical record of one of his demonstration trance inductions, which are different from those he employed later in his teaching seminars in his home.

As an aside, let me point out a problem with interviewing Erickson. He had a way of joining with the person who interviewed him and adapting what he said to the context and person where it was being said. In the many years that John Weakland and I talked with him about therapy and hypnosis, it was necessary to develop what we thought was the best way to bring out his ideas. Of course, at times we offered our own views, but when we wished to have a situation described from Erickson's view, we had to be careful not to first express our own. If we asked whether he did something because of some theory, he was likely to say that was so, with some modifications which he would outline. For example, if he advised a parent to take some action, and we asked if he did that because of conditioning theory, he would talk to us about the incident in terms of conditioning theory. If we merely asked why he did that, or remained silent and waited for him to come up with an explanation, he would offer a quite different and often unique explanation. That is one reason why in my conversations with Dr. Erickson there are long silences. I am waiting for him to come up with his view rather than imposing my own.

In this interview about the film, there is some of that problem. I had studied the film carefully and had certain ideas about why he did something in an induction, but I could not first present those ideas or he might join me in that view. I had to wait until he came up with his reasons and then offer my own version to see what he thought of it. Interviewing Erickson, as with interviewing anyone who thinks in new ways and is trying to find a language for it, requires a special skill and an ability to restrain oneself.

In the room when the film was played were Erickson, myself, Madeleine Richeport, and Robert Erickson, who was running the projector. The discussion began with some prefatory comments by Erickson.

*Erickson:* The film itself is incomplete. There are sections cut out here and there. Where perhaps I had an arm lift and lower and lift again, and alternate right and left, they might have put in the right, they might have put in part of the right and left alternation. There were certain remarks omitted. Some of them I can recall, in part. Another important thing is that at the time I did that I was exceedingly ill. There were only two people at the meeting that thought I could function. Everybody said I couldn't function. But Ravitz and Yanovski said if Erickson said he can do it, he can do it. I had only this memory of the situation: of crossing that basement room in a wheel chair, working with a number of subjects, and Bertha Rogers' worried face. She was fearful I would fall flat on my face. And the knowledge that there was a lot of distracting noise. And that Dr. A was very resentful that I was on the program. I remember being wheeled part way across that room, and my next memory is being in a taxi cab leaving Philadelphia. Then the next memory is being somewhere on the way to Phoenix, possibly this side of the Mississippi. So what I will remember of the film will be as choppy as the film itself. There are certain things that I can say. And when I say "stop," you stop it.

THE FILM IS PLAYED

*(There is a stage. On the left is a table where 4 volunteer subjects and Mrs. Erickson [who later demonstrated self-hypnosis] are sitting, waiting to take their turns. In this demonstration, the volunteers happen to be all female. On the right, in view of the subjects, Erickson sits facing a young woman subject.)*

*E Film:* **Tell me have you ever been in an hypnotic trance before?**
*Subject #1:* **No.**
*E Film:* **Have you ever seen one?**
*Subject #1:* **No.**
*E Film:* **Do you know what it's like to go into a hypnotic trance?**
*Subject #1:* **No.**

*Erickson:* Before that girl came up I had looked them over (the five women subjects sitting at the table). And all of them didn't realize that I had looked at each one separately. And then, this isn't an actual memory, it's a knowledge. I selected one who was not at the front end of the line. I selected one who was in perhaps the second or the third seat. So they were totally unexpected. When she first sat down in the chair, I said, "Hi." Now in a scientific meeting where someone is on exhibition, there is a certain amount of self-consciousness. I had said the word "Hi." I not only said it to the girl but to the entire group. "Hi." Then I repeated it more than once. They cut out the "Hi" with some of the last subjects. You don't say "Hi" to somebody in front of a serious audience, you say "Hi" when it's a strictly personal thing. You limit the area to be dealt with. People don't know that, but you personalize the situation by saying "Hi." And that had the effect of isolating the subject from the situation.

*Haley:* How much of what you say to this first girl, or to the others, is also being said to the other ladies on the platform?

*Erickson:* All of it is being said, and then there are certain repetitions because the other girls will say, "That can't happen to me." Therefore you have to have it happen to them. Like lifting the arm. And that gives all of them a realization that hypnosis is possible. Not only for me, but for you and the other fellow.

*Haley:* Your first statement here was, "Have you ever been in a trance before?" Was that to establish the premise that she was already in one?

*(Often Erickson would communicate double meanings, or puns, deliberately. He had once pointed out to me that when he asked, "Have you been in a trance before?" he was suggesting that the person was in a trance now, while appearing to be making a simple query about whether she had experienced it before.)*

*Erickson:* No. I had never met these girls. I made the remarks to that effect, and I had never met them. My first sight of them was when I was in a wheel chair being wheeled to the back of that room, the adjacent room. They had all looked at me, they all knew they were on exhibition on closed television to an audience upstairs. They were aware of the plumbers that were pounding on the pipes around. And the television crew. And they knew there were a lot of people thinking various thoughts. Some of which thoughts in nursing would not be desirable thoughts. (*The volunteers were probably nurses.*) So I had to personalize it. I asked all of them had they ever been in a trance before, because I had specified I wanted to know if any of them had been in a trance. I wanted them to be free to tell me so. But I also wanted to know which ones had previous experience so I could do things more rapidly.

*E Film:* **Did you know that you do all the work, and I just sit by and enjoy watching you work?**
*Subject #1:* **No, I didn't know that.**
*E Film:* **You didn't know that. Well, I'm really going to enjoy watching you work.**

*Erickson:* "I am going to enjoy watching you work." Which actually means *you* are going to work and I am going to enjoy it. It's a displacement that can't be recognized. And of course you don't mind if I enjoy watching you work.

*E Film:* **Now the first thing I'm going to do is this. I'm going to take hold of your hand and lift it up. It's going to lift up, like that. (Erickson lifts her hand.) And you can look at it. (He lets go and her hand remains up.)**

*Erickson:* And watch the movement of my hands. You lift the hand. You first put a reasonable but recognizable pressure on the hand. Then while you're still lifting it, you stop the lifting and you bring about a directing sensation. Start the hand lifting, and then (demonstrating a lifting touch) and that indicates "go higher." But they can't analyze that, and then you can slide your hand off slowly so they aren't quite certain just when your hand left contact with theirs. There is a state of uncertainty. So that they really don't know, "Is my hand being touched or is it free from contact?" And that state of bewilderment allows you to say anything you wish to introduce something else. Because people don't know how to deal with that question. Either you have hold of it or you don't have hold of it, but when you don't know, "Am I holding it or am I not holding it?" And that period of time extends in their reaction.

*E Film:* **And close your eyes and go deeply, soundly asleep. So deeply, so soundly asleep, so deeply so soundly asleep that you could undergo an operation, that anything legitimate could happen to you.**

*Erickson:* Ordinarily I would tell her "so deeply so soundly asleep," and then I would look away, and the audience would get the impression that I had abandoned the subject to get back into contact with them, that I was leaving her there alone. That would convey the message, "She alone is doing this." And the subject – as Betty mentioned later (when she demonstrated self hypnosis) – that she heard me breathing. Has anyone in this room heard anybody breathe? There has been a lot of breathing done, but nobody heard it. But Betty heard it. And the subject heard my breathing, and she knows that my breathing came from a different direction when I turned my head. A breathing sound is altered.

In the technique of hand levitation, "Your hand is lifting higher and higher and higher," your voice is going up. It may be the same tonal quality, but the locus is going up higher and higher, and you're giving the suggestion in a verbal fashion and in the locus fashion. And often when the subject fails to respond to hand levitation, you can start the moving higher and higher and higher, and they'll respond to the rising locus of your voice. The audience doesn't know anything about that. They're just paying attention to the words. Then if the subject still fails to levitate the hand, you can heighten the tone of your words. You can get higher (demonstrating voice rising higher) and higher, which is an exaggeration (his inflection). I can't do that very well, but those with good musical knowledge do it automatically. They don't know it, but if you listen to a very competent person you see that they alter the tone of the voice and they do get higher in the tonal qualities of the voice. So you've got an observable phenomenon. And to others, one is not observed and one which is disregarded, and you've got a multiple manner of suggestion.

And in psychotherapy when you say to your patient, "You can forget about that sort of thing." What have you done? You have been talking to the patient, "You can forget about that sort of thing." (He turns his head.) You are talking about that sort of thing over there. Which has nothing to do with the person. You move it. People respond so nicely to that. The magician distracts your attention, he takes the rabbit out of his robe and puts it in the hat because you are looking at some unessential movement he's making over here. It's a displacement technique, a displacement at a vocal level and at a verbal level. Nobody notices it, but the unconscious does. (As an aside he discusses the toilet training of children in terms of their learning conscious planning to make it to the bathroom.)

Haley: You put the emphasis on her doing the work. Was there something about her that made you decide to do that?

*(Often the hypnotist suggests that the subject is going to do all the work as a way of reassuring an uneasy subject. It is a suggestion that she will be in charge*

*of what happens, and the hypnotist will be a follower. Usually this is considered a special technique, but there are hypnotists who take it as a philosophy and consider hypnosis to be a situation where the subject is put in charge. Sometimes, techniques become "schools" when they are misunderstood. In this case my assumption that he was making the subject feel more at ease was not his stated purpose, but he emphasized the larger social context indirectly to make the other subjects feel at ease.)*

*Erickson:* That was to distract the other subjects from the discovery that even while waiting for me they were going to respond to whatever I said to the girl. So I made it very apparent it was she and she alone, so that they could give their attention to that and would not pay attention to what was occurring to them. Because there is a tendency when you know you are going to be a subject. Now you've met Dr. B, haven't you? The first time I met Dr. B she was underweight, she was timid, uncertain, and insecure. She attended a seminar. I looked over the audience. I sighted Dr. B as a subject. I put six chairs on the platform. I got five volunteers. And then I said, "This sixth chair might as well be occupied by someone. How about you?" I addressed Dr. B. I spoke a few words to the first subject and dismissed her from the platform. There were just two on the platform. You could almost see Dr. B realize that *she* was going to be the subject. It was a slow progression. There are five left, four left, I'm going to four, three left, two left. I dismissed four. (Inaudible phrase.) All of those who were dismissed sat at the side of me. So it was obvious who was the subject. And Dr. B became a very responsive subject. She didn't know that the greater part of my technique in inducing a trance was dismissing the other subjects. And people aren't aware of that sort of thing. The carnival worker is. The carne works that way. A magician works that way. And we all learn it.

Another thing is you become aware of sound. A baby first hears sound. He doesn't know where it comes from. But you learn to recognize eventually sound from below, from above, from the side, in front, in back, in all possible places. Only you don't know that you do that. You can be in a room and you sense something and you look up there. How did you learn to look up there instead of here? And you watch people doing that. This learning of the locus of sound is a very important thing, and I employed that with all the subjects by turning. As I say, I was sick, and I was very careful to keep in contact with the situation. My turns were slow, deliberate, and I made my turns with relocation of my voice very extensive. But it was a hard thing to explain to that audience because they couldn't comprehend the importance of that. But I knew it was important. I knew that I was very sick and that I better be pretty careful in the direction of the patient's attention, visual attention, auditory attention, in some exaggerated fashion. And so much of my behavior was exaggerated.

*E Film:* **Now I'm going to surprise you, but that's all right. (Erickson takes her ankle and uncrosses her leg.) I will be very very careful about it.**

*(It is so unusual for a hypnotist to touch a woman's ankle that it deserves some comment. Hypnosis deals with one of the most important questions in human life: How much power will I let someone have over me? It is in the nature of power that it is threatening since one might be exploited by the person with power. It is also appealing because it is protective and being taken care of is a positive experience. Erickson plays with all aspects of power in his hypnotic work. He gets out from under power by saying the young woman will do all the work of hypnosis while he enjoys watching her work. Then he says he is going to surprise her, but he will be careful about it. Previously he has said that only legitimate things will be done to her. This is a combination of threat (a man touching her ankle) and protection (when he says he will be careful about it). The combination of protection and threat intensifies any relationship. Discussing this action, Erickson has his own unique view.)*

*Erickson:* "I will be very very careful. " Just when did I touch the leg? You can't see it on the film. "I will be very very careful." Careful was followed by me making contact with her leg. Now who was to be careful, she or I? And in that state of doubt all became my favor. You notice she couldn't take the idea, "What's the idea of touching my leg?" She had to start with the word careful and the doctor and not with the meaningfulness of the touch.

*Haley:* Why did you want to move her leg?

*Erickson:* I wanted to demonstrate to the audience that a total stranger in front of an audience could take hold of a lady's leg and produce a catalepsy. And do it without any preliminary discussion and do it easily, naturally. Because in teaching hypnosis you want to teach the accuracy, the casualness, without letting them know how casual and how uncasual it is. How careful it is.

*E Film:* **And are you comfortable?**

*Erickson:* "And are you comfortable?" Yes. very comfortable. Nodding yes. Others don't realize it and don't recognize it. But all our lives we have been conditioned to respond to that sort of thing, only we don't know it.

*E Film:* **And you can nod your head again. Do you know how the ordinary**

person nods his head? You really don't, but they nod it this way
(nodding his head up and down rapidly). And you nod it this way
(slowly nodding).

*Erickson:* She nodded her head. Now watch closely. She nodded her head
and then there was a perseveration of the movement. In the ordinary
waking state you nod your head and then you stop. In the hypnotic
state you nod your head at whatever speed is comfortable for you, and
then there is a slight perseveration which tells the experienced operator
how well in the trance the subject is.

*E Film:* You don't know what I'm talking about but that's all right. And
now your hand is going to lift up toward your face. (Erickson lifts her
hand.) And you didn't really know that it was that easy, did you? And
when it touches your face you'll take a deep breath and go way deep
sound asleep.

*Erickson:* You'll take a deep breath and go way sound asleep. If you take
the first step, you can make the second step. So you emphasize the
first step by "When you touch you will take a deep breath." The
emphasis is all put on the second step, and they can safely take the
first step without realizing that they are thus being conditioned to take
the second step.

*E Film:* And you didn't know it would be that easy, did you? And it is so
far different from the show-off stage hypnosis, isn't it?

*Erickson:* And you proceed minimally there, but you can recognize it.

*E Film:* Because you realize that you're the one who is really doing it. You
know that, do you not. I am going to ask you to open your eyes. (She
opens her eyes.) Hi. Have you been in a trance?

*(Erickson begins a series of awakenings with this subject. Each time he awakens
her, it is in such a way as to encourage amnesia. The "Hi" and the question he asks
are appropriate behavior if she has just sat down. These encourage her to respond
as if that is so, thereby forgetting what has previously happened The way he does
it is more evident with later awakenings.)*

*Erickson:* The "Hi" there is reinforcing the distance between us two. That's
all. And the subject doesn't become alarmed when they discover they
are all alone, and there is only one other person there, because they still
have some memory of being surrounded by a large number of people

and they are not startled by suddenly finding themselves all alone in a vacuum. The "Hi" reduces it.

*Subject #1:* **I don't know.**
*E Film:* **You don't? You really don't know. I'll tell you the way to find out. Watch your eyelids to see if they start closing on you.**

*Erickson:* How do you watch eyelids? You've got to move them in order to watch them. The subject doesn't have the time or the sophistication to know that you have to move the eyelids to watch them. It's what could be called an unfair, a sneaky way of getting across a suggestion without making a suggestion. Betty and I were trying to figure out one night what word was appropriate to giving a suggestion without giving a suggestion. Deviousness? How can you really describe that? We couldn't find a single word in the dictionary that seemed to fit.

*E Film:* **And if they start closing on you that will mean that you've been in a trance. And down they go, that's beautiful, down they go, down they go. That's right. All the way now. And all the way. All the way until they stay shut.**

*Erickson:* "Until." If you accept the word "until" you are also accepting the word "shut" only that isn't recognized or realized "until." When does "until" end? At the subject's own choice of time. And when should a patient reach a certain weight? Not until it's reasonable. The patient can then set a date. When you say, "Let's be reasonable." And if they don't make the weight on the selected date. "Let's be reasonable" has been said. A patient does not despair. The patient can then extend the period of time. In all therapy it's that way.

*E Film:* **And now all that proof came from within you, did it not? And you can talk and, you can understand me. And you can hear. And you can obey instructions. For example, if I ask you to lift your right arm, you can lift your right arm.**

*(Ordinarily Erickson informs subjects that they can talk and understand when he considers them in a quite deep trance and wishes not to lose contact with them. Another aspect of this comment is Erickson's curious use of metaphor. Usually, when one says "for example," it is not a directive but a general statement about a hypothetical situation. What Erickson does is make the general statement and then give it as a directive. That is, it is nonthreatening to listen to "for example" since nothing is going to be asked of one, but in that frame Erickson requests an action.)*

*Erickson:* "And you can obey instructions." The question is what instructions? That's a threat. To counter the threat you raise your arm and also preface it with the same, "You can hear," "You can feel." When it comes to doing "for example," raise your arm. You can do physically anything, only people don't understand that at a conscious level.

*Haley:* "For example" then is an item in a class, and the rest of the class goes along with it, is what you mean.

*Erickson:* Yes.

**E *Film:* (Erickson demonstrates by lifting his right arm with his left one, and she lifts her arm.) Slowly lifting up. Now it's stopped.**

*Haley:* Why did it lift that fast?

*Erickson:* You can back that film up, and if you were to listen to my voice, I think you would notice a greater rapidity in my speech. "And your hand can lift faster." That's exaggerated. And get that effect.

**E *Film:* It's slowly lifting. Now it stopped. And no matter what you try to do it stays right there. And really try hard to put it down. (Her arm jerks slightly downward.)**

*(The use of the "challenge" is typical in hypnosis, and Erickson uses many varieties from subtle suggestions to forceful requirements. Essentially, the message is, "I want you to obey me by demonstrating that you cannot disobey me." It can be a frightening experience not to be able to control one's arm, and Erickson follows this with a characterization of it as charming and interesting.)*

*Erickson:* And now I'm talking to *you*. I stay right there leaning forward which says, "I'm talking to *you*." And emphasizing that interpersonal relationship.

**E *Film:* The first time in your whole life that you ever experienced such difficulty lowering your hand. Isn't that right?**
*Subject #1:* **Mmm. (smiling)**
**E *Film:* Isn't it charming? Isn't it interesting?**
*Subject #1:* **Mmhmm.**
**E *Film:* That's right.**

*Erickson:* There's a cut there.

*Haley:* What do you think was cut?

*Erickson:* I told her to sense a feeling from her hand lowering. I know that from what I said there. I don't remember it. But it's obvious that I told

her to sense the feeling of her hand lowering, and as she lowered it
and sensed it, it went in a jerky fashion.

*E Film:* **That's right.**

*Erickson:* What's right? It applies to all that she is doing but you're not
saying everything you are doing is right. You're just saying, "It's right."
But she automatically applies it to everything she does. And you say,
"That's right, Johnny." He feels he's sitting right, standing right,
walking right, writing right, everything. Information or narrowing it,
focusing it. Except that we don't really realize that we do that. Your
contact with Birdwhistell *(an authority on body movement)* ought to tell you
a lot about that.

*E Film:* **You'll believe that you've been in a trance, if I have you open your**
**eyes and wake up wide awake? I'd like to have you believe that you**
**can't be hypnotized. Is that all right?**
*Subject #1:* **Yes.**
*E Film:* **You know, you can't really be hypnotized, and as soon as you**
**open your eyes you'll know that.**

*(Many years ago when I was on Gregory Bateson's project on communica-*
*tion, he formulated the idea of the double bind. It was defined as a paradoxical*
*communication situation where a message at one level conflicted with a message*
*at another level, and the person had to respond and could not leave the field.*
*A classic example was the directive where one person says to another, "Disobey*
*me." The subject can neither disobey nor obey, because disobeying means obey-*
*ing. Our problem after discovering this paradox was in finding one in human*
*relations. One of the first examples I found was in hypnosis. In the nature of*
*the situation the hypnotist directs the subject to spontaneously respond. How*
*can one respond spontaneously on command? There were also specific directives*
*often used in hypnosis that were obvious binds, and one classic one is present*
*here. Erickson gives the subject a post hypnotic suggestion to say she can't be*
*hypnotized. She faces a paradox: if she follows the posthypnotic suggestion, she*
*is in a trance. Therefore, saying she can't be hypnotized is saying she was*
*hypnotized. If she does not follow the suggestion and says she can't be hypnotized,*
*then she is conceding she was hypnotized. She must admit she was hypnotized*
*no matter what she does.)*

*Erickson:* She can't open her eyes until she *knows* that.
*Haley:* Come around with that again?
*Erickson:* She can't open her eyes until she *knows* that. "As soon as you
open your eyes you'll know that you can't be hypnotized." She opens

her eyes, and that means that she knows she can't be. It's an indirect suggestion without it being recognized.

*E Film:* **Tell me, do you think you can be hypnotized?**
*Subject #1:* **No, I don't.**
*E Film:* **You really don't.**
*Subject #1:* **No.**
*E Film:* **I'd like to have you explain this one little thing. (He lifts her right hand, and it stays up in the air.) And did you ever have a strange man lift your hand and leave it in mid-air like that before?**
*Subject #1:* **No. (smiling)**
*E Film:* **Do you know that in hypnosis, in medical hypnosis, sometimes you want a patient to hold very, very still. So that you can do an operation, do all manner of things with the patient's full cooperation. And you know during an operation you haven't got time to explain to a patient exactly what they should do. For example, if I told you to close your eyes, you could close them. *Now.* (Her eyes blink and then stay closed.)**

*Erickson:* You can see her beginning to understand.

*E Film:* **You can close them so nicely, and keep them closed so nicely. And surgically that might be a most important thing. The immobility of your right arm might be a most important thing surgically. Now you know medical hypnosis is far different from stage hypnosis. Stage hypnosis is where somebody throws out his chest and widens his eyes...**

*Erickson:* That explanation was for the benefit of the audience as well as for the other subjects. And I'm talking to all of the subjects there. So I was reassuring the subjects. And I'm reassuring the audience.

*(Erickson mentions stage hypnosis in this demonstration more often than he usually does. He spent his life opposing hypnotic charlatanism and differentiating it from medical hypnosis.)*

*E Film:* **(continuing) ...and tells the audience what a great man he is. But what I would like to have you understand is that you as a person are really a very great person able to do a lot of things that will help you medically. Does that make you feel happy?**

*(Erickson typically rewarded subjects for volunteering at his demonstrations, as will be discussed later.)*

*Subject #1:* **Yes.**

*E Film:* **Now I don't know what your future is going to be, but I hope that if you ever get married and have a baby, that you can have it very comfortably and easily...**

*Erickson:* "I hope if you ever get married and you have a baby you will have it comfortably." I'm not just talking to her. I mean everybody. Because that meant I am talking to *all* within my vision.

*E Film:* **(continuing) ...if you have an operation you can have it comfortably and easily, that any surgery that you can have will be comfortable and easily. Any dental work that you have will be comfortable and easily. Does that seem agreeable to you?**

*Erickson:* And having talked to the general audience, I can now talk to the subject directly and the audience will naturally remain my audience.

*Subject #1:* **Very.**
*E Film:* **Very?**
*Subject #1:* **Yes.**
*E Film:* **I'm so glad of that. And I hope you'll keep that knowledge with you for all the rest of your life. And it isn't really ever important for you to know that I hypnotized you, the important thing is for you to know that you did it all by yourself. I'd like to have you take one or two or three deep breaths and wake up wide awake.**

*Erickson:* And I saw her make the waking up her own process. "One or two deep breaths. And wake up wide awake." She opened her mouth slightly. Parted her eyelids. Continues the elevation of her head. Altered her breathing. That was all done by her. Also, I emphasized there in an exaggerated fashion, all the hypnosis occurs within you. It isn't the doctor or the dentist, or psychologist who does it, it is you with a process within yourself. So many doctors when they start hypnotizing, start out thinking they are doing it. And all they are doing is offering suggestions, really hoping the subject will pay attention to at least some of them.

*E Film:* **Hi. Tell me, what is your first name?**

*(Again, Erickson greets the young woman as if she just sat down. Asking her name is appropriate behavior for just meeting. The tendency of the subject is to have amnesia for what had happened in the trance previously.)*

*Subject #1:* **Harriet.**

*E Film:* **Harriet? I think that's a nice name. Would you like to shake hands with me?**

*Subject #1:* **Yes.**

*E Film:* **You would? (Lifts her hand, and it remains up.) You know, shaking hands with me is rather...**

*Erickson:* There you saw me exaggerating the separation of my hand from hers. So the doctors who attended that seminar, that meeting, those that had attended previous seminars had heard me emphasize the importance of minor suggestion, slow actions, and giving the subject time to respond. And giving that time in a way that would not be recognized. So I exaggerated that. And those who had listened to me previously, most of them had, could see it in very exaggerated fashion.

*E Film:* **And did you know that you could go into a trance that quickly and that easily?**

*Subject #1:* **No.**

*E Film:* **You can, can't you, even with your eyes wide open. You know, if you want to you can see just *you* and *me*. And nothing else. Not even the television cameras, the lights or anything else.**

*Erickson:* You know when I say, "You know you can see just you and me," she didn't check up on it. There's no tendency to look and see. She accepted the word unquestionably. And when you don't question a thing, you accept it.

*Haley:* If you wanted to rule out the television cameras and such, why do you name them to her?

*Erickson:* For those sophisticated, you name them. Does she make a response to their names ? For example, if I was writing here. She was aware that she was sitting beside the cedar chest and the television. Even though you tried to control it, you made a minimal turn. (laughs) In hypnosis they don't. It's so hard, there's nothing more insulting to a person. Medical students often tried to heckle me. And it was perfectly obvious that I thought that chap was sitting there heckling me but there was something over there (looking beyond him). And you could see the heckling dwindle down and down. (laughs) And when someone tries to be insulting, you look elsewhere. And the guy who is trying to insult you says, "Why doesn't he look at me?" He's pretty helpless. And you can cut him down so easily, so quickly. You can practice that on your kids, you know. Isn't that right, Robert? And you do it in teaching, don't you?

*E Film:* **Just me. And you don't have to blink your eyes with normal frequency, or anything of that sort. And your hand and arm feel so comfortable. Now close your eyes. (Harriet closes her eyes.) That's right, all the way. And take a deep breath, and wake up. (Harriet opens her eyes.) Let me shake hands again. (shakes hands) Hi. Harriet, I'm so glad to meet you.**

*(Our brains seem to work in such a way that we make social continuities, even if that requires amnesia. In this case Erickson takes the young woman's hand, leans back separating their hands and then does various hypnotic directives. Then he takes her hand again, shaking it, and awakens her. He follows this with, "Hi, Harriet, I'm so glad to meet you," as if they had just sat down together. The actions during the handshake will tend to be forgotten by the subject. One can do the same in therapy with hypnosis by starting a sequence, interrupting it for trance experiences, and then continuing the sequence again, thereby giving amnesia for the trance behavior. Erickson taught me this technique, but he chooses a different aspect of it later when I query him about it.)*

*Erickson:* It's best when you're using hypnosis if the subject has the eyes open, you tell them to close their eyes, and then you tell them to awaken. They've had a lifetime of experience of opening their eyes as a part of the awakening. What they don't realize is they're learning that when they close their eyes they go to sleep.

*Haley:* Were you trying for an amnesia there—is that why you ended the way you started on that handshake?

*Erickson:* Yes. If you want to produce an amnesia, a conscious amnesia, you return to the beginning, and terminate at the beginning. And you'll effect an amnesia that way. You can go into a classroom of medical students, and you can say to them, "I want you to remember very carefully... (voice trailing off) What's going on there. By the way, what did I start to say?" You make an emphatic statement, you interrupt, and you distract their attention. You go back, and surprisingly they have forgotten. "Now I want you to remember!" And when you do that for a class of medical students, for example, as a preliminary to a discussion of hypnosis, to show them that they can be having amnesia induced without hypnosis. Then they are much more susceptible to hypnosis. Because they have been convinced by the normal behavior.

*E Film:* **Thank you so much for helping me.**
*Subject #1:* **Thank you.**
*E Film:* **Do you realize that you really helped me a great deal?**
*Subject #1:* **I have?**
*E Film:* **I've taken away, I hope, a lot of the mystery of stage hypnotists**

**and all the other charlatans trying to put upon hypnosis. Thank you. And I'm very grateful to you. Are you wide awake now?**

*Subject #1:* **Yes.**

*E Film:* **That's good. Now do you suppose we ought to have you change seats with somebody else?**

*Subject #1:* **Yes.**

*E Film:* **All right. (The assistant takes off her microphone.) The girl in the blue dress.**

*Erickson:* I told her to get the lady in the blue dress, because I wasn't going up to the ladies, she was. You ask the subject to bring up somebody. In seminars, how do you deal with resistant subjects? A number will indicate that they are resistant And you call one of them up and let them be resistant. Call the next one by having that subject escort the other person up. And the other person is wondering why he wasn't resistant. By letting the other fellow lead him up, he's transferring his resistance to that person all the way coming up to you. Only they don't realize it.

*(With each of these subjects Erickson uses a different approach. For the next subject he does an essentially Rogerian induction by largely repeating back to her what she says. It is interesting that the Rogerian approach, which is claimed to be only reflective and not directive, can be used to induce someone into an hypnotic trance.)*

*E Film:* **Tell me, have you ever been in a trance before?**

*Subject #2:* **I think so.**

*E Film:* **You think so. (Dr. Erickson leans back, then he leans forward and takes her right hand and lifts it.) And who put you in a trance before?**

*Subject #2:* **Dr. Yanovski.**

*E Film:* **Dr. Yanovski? That was very nice of him.**

*Subject #2:* **I enjoyed it.**

*E Film:* **You enjoyed it. (He leans back while she sits with her hand in the air.) And when do you think you'll go into a trance for me?**

*Subject #2:* **The way my arm feels, I imagine I might be in one now.**

*Erickson:* "And when do you think you'll go into a trance for me?" She'd been in a trance with Yanovski. "And when do you think you'll go into a trance for me?" You start assessing time, physical feelings, previous experience. Then she noticed her arm. And that told her. You can often do that with an inexperienced subject. In the seminars, after the first morning of lectures, I would mingle with the audience, shake hands with them, ask them where they came from. As I shook hands with them, I would slowly withdraw my hand, alter the focus of my eyes as if I were looking past and beyond them, alter the tone of my voice as if I was talking to someone back there. And those who went into a trance, I could see that right away. Then I could shift the tone of my voice, the focus of my eyes, and say something that I had said when they were fully awake and bring them out of the trance. They had been in a trance and didn't know it, they had an amnesia, and when it came time to pick out a subject in the audience, I had already tested them.

Haley: Was there a reason why you waited until you touched her hand and started to lift it before you asked who had hypnotized her before?

Erickson: My timing was wrong. I had a great deal of pain at that time, and my timing was off.

Haley: What should the timing have been?

Erickson: I should have asked the question before I really touched her hand.

Haley: Why is that?

Erickson: She had seen the other girl develop an hypnotic state. By catalepsy. And my timing was wrong. She didn't really have the opportunity to tell me that she had been Yanovski's hypnotic subject before she was in a trance. So I made the best of it, without betraying my error.

E Film: **The way your arm feels you might be in a trance right now. In what way does your arm feel different?**

Subject #2: **It tingles.**

E Film: **It singles. It's apart from you.**

Haley: What is this "singles"?

Erickson: Have you ever had your leg go to sleep? Hypnotically you can get that partial awareness here and there that has the same tingling effect. My speech was slurred.

Haley: That wasn't deliberate?

Erickson: No.

Haley: It comes out clear as a bell "singles."

Erickson: I know.

Haley: I thought you were doing some kind of a word device with her.

Erickson: No, that was slurring of my speech.

Haley: Well I'll be darned. Okay.

Subject #2: **No, it tingles, it tingles, it tingles.**

E Film: **No it just plain singles.**

Subject #2: **No it tingles, my hand... Well now maybe it singles. It doesn't seem to be so much a part of me as it was before.**

Erickson: There I capitalized on "single." "Singles" is a thing apart. I was capitalizing on my slurred speech before.

*E Film:* **Tell me, are your eyes open?**
*Subject #2:* **Wide open**
*E Film:* **You're sure of that?**
*Subject #2:* **Right now I am.**
*E Film:* **Right now you are. Are you still being sure of it?**
*Subject #2:* **Yes.**
*E Film:* **Are they closing?**
*Subject #2:* **Not yet.**
*E Film:* **You're sure?**
*Subject #2:* **Yes. (Her lids drop.)**
*E Film:* **All the way. All the way. And stay shut. All the way. All the way.**

*Erickson:* As you watch that eyelid behavior. She shows it very nicely. The fluctuation of her desires. Shall she keep them open or shall she let them close? So she had closed her eyes. She closes them all the way and then opens them and then closes them all the way or opens them halfway. "Oh hell, let's let them go all the way shut and stay shut." That's what she did.

*E Film:* **Stay shut now. (Her eyes remain closed.)**

*Erickson:* You also notice I didn't offer any suggestions. I offered only questions. They were questions intended to raise a doubt, an uncertainty, and at the same time, my lack of suggestion, my expression of curiosity, of interest me to her, might begin to question, "Are my eyes going to close?" The only way she is going to find out if they are going to close is by closing them. And she doesn't know that's the only way she can find out.

*E Film:* **Take a deep breath and go way deep into a trance. And in any future hypnosis, whether medical or dental, I hope you'll enjoy it thoroughly, and I hope that never never will you use hypnosis to entertain people but to instruct them and make them much more aware. Do you mind if I talk about you?**
*Subject #2:* **No.**
*E Film:* **It doesn't make you self-conscious, does it?**
*Subject #2:* **No. Not when you're in trance.**

*Erickson:* I knew I was thinking that our Society knew I was sick. They were all in doubt about it. I better acknowledge to the audience that I knew it too. So I exaggerated the movement of my arm so they got the message without knowing it. Von looked at it and said, "Why the hell did you have to advertise that you were sick?" He understood.

*E Film:* **But you can make response to me. Isn't that right?**
*Subject #2:* **Yes, I can.**
*E Film:* **And all of your surroundings seem awfully unimportant, do they not?**
*Subject #2:* **That's right. I'm only conscious of your voice.**
*E Film:* **You're only conscious of my voice. That's enough, isn't it really?**
*Subject #2:* **Oh, yes.**
*E Film:* **You're here for a medical purpose to demonstrate various things. And so take a deep breath and rouse up completely rested and refreshed and energetic. (She opens her eyes.) Do you think you're wide awake?**
*Subject #2:* **Well. (pause) No, I don't. I can't get my arm down.**
*E Film:* **You can't get your arm down.**
*Subject #2:* **No.**
*E Film:* **You mean your arm is still asleep?**

*Erickson:* Now there I lifted her arm apart from actual induction of trance. I mistimed when I induced a trance before I wanted a trance. So when I awakened her I awakened her in relationship to a trance induction that occurred in the lifting of her arm. In other words, two different trance states had been established, and she had to awaken in both of them. And I let her demonstrate that she awakened, but she couldn't really be because her hand was still up. She couldn't get it down. And that segmentation of the body is so important in the matter of hypnosis, in medicine, and in dentistry, and color vision experiments, psychological experiments of all kinds. The matter of psychotherapy, you separate things.
*Haley:* Did you anticipate that? You were that aware?
*Erickson:* Oh, yes, I was aware.

*(The two trances that Erickson refers to are done in a special way if one looks carefully at the film. The question is why the woman's arm stays up when she has been awakened. It might be that he did not awaken her but only appeared to. For example, he might say, "I want you to wake up?" with a slight questioning inflection which the subject will hear, although an audience might not. That question turns a directive into an inquiry. However, in this case he did not suggest awakening in that way. Another explanation is possible when assuming there were two trances involved. They can be described in a series of stages. First, Erickson asks the woman if she has been hypnotized before, and she says, "I think so." Second, Erickson reaches out and takes her hand and lifts it. As he does so, he asks who previously put her in a trance. She says, "Dr. Yanovski." Third, Erickson leans back and says, "And when do you think you will go into a trance for me?" It appears that when Erickson heard the woman had been previously hypnotized he assumed that*

*if one recalls a previous trance in an hypnotic situation there is a tendency to go back into that trance. Therefore, Erickson took that opportunity to make a trance through association with the previous hypnotist and a separate trance of his own. The lifted arm was part of the trance of the previous hypnotist. Therefore, when Erickson awakened her from his trance, she was still in the trance of the previous hypnotist. What is impressive is how rapidly Erickson made the decision to make use of the previous trance and separate it from his own.)*

*E Film:* **Let's change things. Let's have the other arm asleep. (He lifts her left arm and the right one drops.) How does that feel?**
*Subject #2:* **That feels like the other one did now.**
*E Film:* **That feels like the other one did. Are your eyes wide awake?**
*Subject #2:* **Yes, I think they are?**
E Film: **You think they are?**
*Subject #2:* **Right now I am.**
*E Film:* **You're beginning to have doubts?**
*Subject #2:* **Well in this kind of thing you always have doubts. (Her lids lower.)**
*E Film:* **You always have doubts. And so when the doctor says, "I doubt if you have pain," what's your reaction?**
*Subject #2:* **(pause) I don't know. I don't suffer from pain very much.**
*E Film:* **Isn't that nice?**
*Subject #2:* **I think it's wonderful.**

*Erickson:* She's educating them by her behavior.
*Haley:* What?
*Erickson:* She is educating the viewers by her own behavior. And when the doctor doubts the pain, can you doubt it? It's nice. You can doubt it. And you can see the change in her eyelid movements. And you could recognize that you could be responding to what was being said even though they were not emphatic, you can really be free from pain which is the wrong way of doing it. You raise a doubt. "Having pain?" The asthmatic child who had psychosomatic asthma. You say to him, "You know you have asthma, and it's hard to breathe. Maybe some of that asthma comes from your discomfort and your fear. You probably wouldn't notice it if only five percent came from fear. You probably wouldn't notice it if only 10 percent came just from fear and not from allergic responses. It would be nice to notice that you had only 80 percent due to allergies. You forget about the 20 percent that comes from your fear." And that makes them feel comfortable.

I did that for a 12-year-old boy. His parents were spending 150 dollars a month for medication the family physician prescribed. And for a couple of weeks the boy got along with only about 10 percent of his asthma. And his parents got so alarmed because he wasn't using the medication, he was breathing comfortably. They told him there was something wrong because he really did have a very bad case of asthma. The parents looked at each other, they told me later. "It was our alarm. We frightened our son to death." And I said, "Yes." The parents said, "You told us that that boy can be comfortable and be pleased." We all make mistakes. One thing you don't know is how much damage his asthma has done to his lungs. You really don't know how much emphysema, so why do you take the blame for causing his death? You really don't know if he might not have died. You take the blame right now. You put it very frankly, emphatically, you take the blame now. You really don't know if he might have died from asthma next month. We really don't know how much emphysema he had, whether they killed the kid. In fact, the doctor killed the boy by prescribing that amount of medication. There was nothing they could do about it after the boy was dead. I'm glad they came in to see me afterwards.

*E Film:* **And even when your dentist works on you, you will feel pain?**

*Erickson:* That strained effort that I put into my voice. "Even when your dentist works on you." And even when your obstetrician tells you to bear down. It all relates. You can be comfortable.
*Haley:* Relates to what?
*Erickson:* It all relates to anything severe, you can feel comfortable.

*E Film:* **By the way, are you alone here now? Can you see anybody else?**
*Subject #2:* **No. Not right now I don't.**
*E Film:* **Just me?**
*Subject #2:* **Yes.**
*E Film:* **Is that enough?**
*Subject #2:* **Right now it is. Yes.**
*E Film:* **Right now it is, yes. Now close your eyes and take a deep breath and wake up wide awake all over. All over.**
*Subject #2:* **How can I wake up all over when I can't get my arm down?**
*E Film:* **How can you wake up all over when you can't get your arm down? You know your arm is part of all over. (Her arm falls to her lap.)**

*Haley:* Did you expect that her arm would stay there?
*Erickson:* But she's had the learning experience of discovering that she could awaken with her arm up. And that comes from the hangover of suggestion. The need to pay attention to every bit of a patient's behavior. Now that wasn't intentional on my part. She furnished a good illustration of the importance of seeing everything possible. And the

failure of people to know that "all over" includes their arm as well as their legs. I'll give you a joke. "I'm following your diet, but I didn't lose weight. First I ate breakfast, and then I took the substance that I should have for breakfast" In other words, they take everything they usually take and the diet as well. (Laughter) And that happens so often. That isn't the most ridiculous one that you can find happening. Be sure you wash your right leg carefully. Two weeks later you examine a patient, and you realize you should have said that it is all right to wash the rest of your body. (Laughter) He was washing just the right leg. It's so ridiculous. I've given time to discover that "all over" meant also her arm. But it took time. You see that thinking, understanding, requires time. In just so simple a thing as that.

*Subject #2:* **Now I think I'm awake.**

*E Film:* **Now you think you're awake. You know it was very very nice of you to cooperate with me. You know I don't know how much time I've got so would you pick the lady in, I think that's a pink dress over there? (The assistant removes the microphone from #2. She leaves, and #3 sits down, and the microphone is adjusted.)**

*Erickson:* Did you notice the speed with which that subject got up? She actually rushed up.

*E Film:* **You know I'm not the first person to tell you that you've got pretty blue eyes? You know that, don't you?**

*Subject #3:* **To tell me.**

*E Film:* **That I'm not the first to tell you that.**

*Subject #3:* **No.**

*Erickson:* What is embarrassing? You tell a woman in front of an audience that she has very pretty blue eyes. How does she feel if she knows that she's on exhibition? Cringing. You didn't see any cringing there. That was for the benefit of the more sophisticated. She has already separated herself from the audience. She was attending to me. She didn't know it, but she was already in a trance. And I didn't think I had to do any more to induce a trance. But I did have to meet the needs of the uninformed in the audience.

*E Film:* **You know the astonishing thing is that pretty blue eyes can be awfully, awfully hard to keep open. Take a deep breath and go way deep sound asleep. In orthopedic surgery the most important thing is to have a patient be able to hold an arm or a leg comfortably in an awkward position hour after hour, day after day. I'd like you to feel** your hand as anesthetic and comfortable as can be. (He lifts her right hand which remains in mid air.) Your arm feels comfortable, does it not?

*Subject #3:* **Very comfortable.**

*E Film:* **Very comfortable.**

*Erickson:* I don't know whether it was in relation to what was done in England or not, but the question of awkward positions and fatigue and medical needs. An English orthopedist was using hypnosis to do a skin graft on an ankle. And with the patient in the trance state he explained the importance of getting the skin graft from the abdomen and keeping his ankle over the abdomen. A terribly broken ankle. And the patient maintained that state for over two weeks. Very carefully done. It was a necessary graft but he could have been strapped into position as was ordinarily done. The question arose: could it have been done under hypnosis without benefit of a cast, the straps, and so on, and maintained during the sleeping state? The patient is able to keep in that awfully awfully awkward position for two weeks.

There are so many things that can be done that people don't know they can be done and won't believe can be done and have to be shown that it can be done. Like what do you call that? Enlarge your right hand and shrink your left hand. How do you do that? You increase the flow of blood to the right hand and delay the flow from it, and you decrease the flow of blood from the left hand and increase the flow away from it. And you watch it on the chart. The right hand gets larger and the left hand gets smaller. It sounds so ridiculous, and yet it's in a physiological laboratory. You close the hands around a container that will maintain a volume and will show changes in increase in volume. And it's surprising how medical students will try to find some way and reluctantly agree that it did happen. You have them do it. The hand is in. You tell them you do exactly as Joe did. And tell them convincingly in the waking state. Then explain you know what the sense of cold is, what the sense of warmth is. And you can let your right hand get cold. You can let the right hand get hot. That will increase the size. Just wait and watch. And then discover that it happened to them even in the waking state. It's so hard to believe people.

And I've produced some anesthesia with Dr. Mead, doctor of physiology. He said, "That's just a pretense, a simulated anesthesia." He spent the next two hours trying to prove there was no anesthesia. Two hours of hard work by himself and the associate professor who admitted, "Now I'll have to learn something about physiology." It was anesthetic. Then they started to check up on medical texts to find out what information there was on where anesthesia actually occurs. Since then a lot was done at the University of Michigan on the nervous system and anesthesia as in large part a central phenomenon and not a local phenomenon.

*E Film:* **Very comfortable. And you haven't lost your ability to talk, your ability to speak. By the way, are just you and I here? (E leans forward with his knee touching hers.)**

*Subject #3:* **Just you and I.**

*E Film:* **Just you and I are here. It's nice to be alone with you, I think it's delightful to be with you. And I'd like to have you enjoy sleeping deeper and sounder...**

*Erickson:* How advisable was it for me to tell a pretty girl in front of an audience, "I want you to enjoy being alone with me, enjoy sleeping." (Laughs) You wouldn't get by with that very easily, would you? But she didn't seem to notice it. Yet that was a very loaded remark. I had a comment on that later, months later. "How did you know you could get by with such a loaded remark?" Some of my friends said they got awfully uncomfortable when I said that. And that's when many realized that in hypnosis you can establish a sense of comfort if you don't violate the person in any way. I was speaking about comfort, aloneness, not about "you and meness." Aloneness and comfort. You and me is a totally different thing. But aloneness, together, and comfort, and sleeping. All of those are comfortable words. And the setting in which something is said gives it that meaning. Not just the word itself. The story about the mother who reproved her son saying, "Damn it, that hurt." The mother said, "Why did you swear?" "Well, it hurt that much." She said, "God damn it, it didn't hurt that much." There's a difference between "God damn it" and "God damn it." And you find that quite often, frequently in social situations.

*Richeport:* I'm curious to know if you're in a trance working with any of these subjects.

*Erickson:* Why do you ask the question?

*Richeport:* I'm curious to know if at any time when you're working with any patients or in this type of situation, if you find there is a personal advantage to put yourself in trance. If you feel that you learn certain things about the other person.

*Erickson:* It's very fortunate that you're here. Jay Haley wants to know and learn. You can watch my movements you will notice that most of them are indicative of a state of hypnosis. I'm free to go in and come out and move back and forth. And in your own study you've seen that. I had the opportunity of demonstrating before an audience Sector was in a trance and didn't know it. Herschman was in a trance but didn't know it.

Thompson was in a trance and didn't know it, Bob Pearson was in a trance but didn't know it. They could demonstrate it so it could be recognized by others, you could point to behavior, see trance behavior that comes and goes, and you can notice it all through here.

*E Film: (continuing)* **I don't want you ever ever to forget the capacity of your body to do a great variety of things. And your arm feels comfortable, doesn't it?**
*Subject#3:* **Very comfortable.**
*E Film:* **And you know, if that arm starts lowering, the other one starts lifting, and there isn't a thing you can do about it. (Her right hand lowers and her left hand rises.)**

*Erickson:* They cut a section there.

*E Film:* **Now one can call that a compulsion, or one can call it some kind of a habit, some kind of a motor response. Would you mind opening your eyes and looking at me? Isn't it astonishing that you and I should be here alone?**
*Subject #3:* **Yes.**

*Haley:* Why do you phrase it that way, Milton, "Isn't it astonishing that...?"
*Erickson:* That's for the benefit of the audience. A failure of the subject to respond to the word astonishing. There is nothing astonishing. There is nothing, absolutely nothing. You can only be astonished to be alone here if you see others here. Now if you're totally unaware of anything, then there is nothing astonishing. You have to have something to cause the astonishment.

*E Film:* **Have we ever been introduced?**
*Subject #3:* **Never.**
*E Film:* **Never? What is your name?**
*Subject #3:* **Susan.**
*E Film:* **Susan. My name is Milton. You know my mother gave me that name. A long time ago.**

*Haley:* Now what are you going into here?
*Erickson:* Von says it's corny. I pointed out you can be very corny and ridiculous, but you're awfully alone, there's only the two of you, nobody else there, and she can't feel embarrassed, no matter how corny I get. Because there's nobody else. It's a separate kind of situation. Your very question says that you are responding in a totally different way. Von's denunciation of that as too damn corny.

*Subject #3:* **It's a nice name.**
*E Film:* **What's that?**
*Subject #3:* **It's a nice name.**
*E Film:* **It is? Well, she liked it too. And I've sort of gotten used to it. And so it's a nice name so far as I'm concerned. And then it's easy to write.**

*Erickson:* (Laughing) How ridiculous can you be? Without eliciting a feeling, "That's ridiculous."

*Haley:* What is your purpose in doing that?

*Erickson:* Of showing that the—Let me say that that situation isn't in context with anything else. It's in context only with her and with me. It would be ridiculous if I told Maddy that my name is Milton, it's a nice name, my mother gave it to me, in the context of this room. The context of the presence of others. But we were really alone.

*Richeport:* Could you have said this to the previous subject?

*Erickson:* Yes.

*Richeport: (continuing)* The same kind of . . .

*Erickson:* You can say ridiculous things in a context only of—well, it is the entire context, there is no other.

*Haley:* Two or three of us looked at this and decided you were up to something else. And it sounds like a very interesting idea. We decided you were trying to produce regression by first behaving younger yourself, which would provoke her to behave younger, and that would make a regression.

*(When a hypnotist regresses a subject to an earlier age, the subject must place the hypnotist in that earlier time by making the hypnotist some other person. If regressed back to childhood, the subject can make the hypnotist another child, or a teacher perhaps. One explanation of what Erickson is doing here, although it is not his explanation, expresses an extreme interpersonal view. Rather than regress the subject and then be changed himself by the subject, Erickson regresses himself and so forces the subject to become younger to make sense of associating with him. If he is childlike, she must be so too, and in that way he regresses her by regressing himself.)*

*Erickson:* In hypnosis there is always regressed behavior. You can see it there because the behavior is out of context. And it is simplified so very much: "It's a nice name."

*Haley:* "And it's easy to write."

*Erickson:* "My mother gave it to me." "Your eyes are a pretty blue."

*Haley:* You were saying what a young boy would possibly say. "My mother gave me that name, it's an easy name to write."

*Erickson:* And I didn't evoke an adult girl's response, did I? I knew it was safe to do that because first of all...

*Haley:* But you weren't attempting to move her younger or into her past.

*Erickson:* No, I was illustrating the simplicity of the aloneness. Exaggerating having one's own context entirely within itself. And no relationship to anything else, past, present or future.

*E Film:* **By the way, have you noticed anything about me? Why do you suppose I carry this (holding up cane)?**

*Subject #3:* **You have a bad leg?**

*E Film:* **Did you ever see me limp?**

*Subject #3:* **No.**

*E Film:* **Do you suppose this is an affectation?**

*Subject #3:* **No.**

*E Film:* **You know, I had a good friend who called it an affectation for two years. And then they discovered that I limped. And they were so surprised. Tell me, can you keep your eyes open?**

*Erickson:* It's the same thing there. The context is just what you see. Just what she heard, just what I said. It has no relationship with the past or the present or the future. It's in total isolation.

*Haley:* When you arrived, she was up there and watched you use that cane getting from the wheel chair.

*Erickson:* Yes she did, because I did walk from the wheel chair over to the other chair. But she didn't relate the cane to that. It was about the moment only. And in psychotherapy, if you can bring about a suddenness of the moment, of the hour of the day, of the event, you can deal with it much more effectively.

*E Film:* **You sure?**

*Subject #3:* **Mmhmmm.**

*E Film:* **I'm not. That's right. They are closing. (She blinks and closes her eyes.) That's right. Now take a deep breath and feel rested and refreshed and wide awake all over. Will you do that for me? Hi, Susan.**

*Subject #3:* **Hi.**

*E Film:* **Well, it's been nice knowing you. Why do you have your hand up like that?**

*Subject #3:* **I don't know.**

*E Film:* **You don't know.**

*Erickson:* Part of the film was cut out there. I awakened her. She had her eyes open, and I was talking to her, and that heavy hammering was going on (noise of banging pipes). And then there was some heavy hammering going on as she was partially awake and heavy hammering *after* she was awake. They cut out most of that because when she was partially awake she made a partial response to the hammering. When fully awake she turned her head and she looked. She just turned it slightly when she was partially awake because the stimulus had been received. Giving a response to the stimulus was obliterated by the trance so she didn't respond any further.

Another way of illustrating that. You offer a piece of candy to a child, and the child reaches out for it. You can draw your hand back. A child not sophisticated like you reaches out a second time. A Mongolian idiot I offered a piece of candy 150 times, full reaching out 150 times. A diagnosis. No normal person can do that. You can't stand 150 frustrations. When somebody is cussing you out, "What did you say?" You let him have it right in the eye (laughs) "What did you say?" They begin to get so frustrated they say, "Well, hell, forget it."

*E Film:* **That lady in gray. I think it's gray. I haven't worked with you before, have I? (Erickson is looking at another subject.) All right, will you get the lady in gray?**

*Haley:* Milton, this one I thought you dismissed much more brusquely than any of the others.
*Erickson:* The film was cut.
*Haley:* It was because of the cutting that it looks like that?

*E Film:* **(Assistant moves the microphone from #3 to #4).**

*Erickson:* She was very brisk in her movements to get up there. She was eager.

*E Film:* **Now, tell me, how do you like to go into a trance? Quickly and suddenly, all at once without any warning just as if you had a broken leg or a broken arm.**

*Erickson:* Without any warning. That's a threatening word. Did you see her widen her eyes at that threatening word? Did you see the alteration in her breathing? A change in her position, the increased alertness. She was already in a trance. Only she didn't know it, and others couldn't recognize it.
*Haley:* What you are saying there if I could hear you right was that when you say something threatening, you then shift to a "for example," or a metaphor.
*Erickson:* Yes. But here I wanted to illustrate the threatening word "without

any warning." And yet it wasn't a threat.

*Haley:* And then you went right into "for example, if you broke a leg," which was a separate thing then.

*Erickson:* Yes

**E *Film:* You lose that pain immediately. Alright, do so. RIGHT NOW. And in a deep sound trance. And you and I are here all alone. And your broken leg doesn't hurt one little bit, does it? And it isn't going to hurt, is it? And can you see the nurses?**

*Erickson:* The film was cut there too. She did have a broken leg. But she didn't make the response looking to see. There is some facial expression as if to say, "Of course I have."

*Haley:* Well, there's something about this, Milton. You have a way of playing with the edge of a metaphor. You go from "It's like having a broken leg" to "Your broken leg feels better," and you play with what's literal and what's metaphoric in this sort of induction. I gather if there was a piece cut out there then it isn't too clear to me, but it looked like this girl was quite uncertain if she did have a broken leg or not.

*Erickson:* I know. There was too much cut out there to follow the transition. Most of that is ruined. We can only take what we see there.

*Haley:* It's not only in this broken leg but in so many hypnotic suggestions. "Your hand is as heavy as lead," and then it shifts to "It is lead."

*Erickson:* Yes.

*Haley:* You seem to be doing that here, which is a different way of doing it, I thought. Because you were making a whole scene out of it. Because actually if she had a broken leg, there would be a hospital scene. And if this was a medical audience she could look around and see doctors and nurses.

*Erickson:* This was in the basement and the audience was upstairs.

*Haley:* There wasn't an audience sitting in front of this group?

*Erickson:* No.

*Haley:* I misunderstood that.

*Erickson:* It was a television camera and they knew that they were being watched on the TV's upstairs, that there was a whole encirclement of the room so that everybody could see. There was a downstairs audience of plumbers, janitors, hotel workers, nosy butt-ins, stragglers and what not. Dr. A didn't want it and made it so unpleasant. The hotel made it unpleasant for me. When she saw the orderlies they cut out the transition to the nurses, and they cut out the interns coming down the hallway. They cut out the—what do you call that, table for transporting patients from one floor to another? She saw other patients. But that was all cut out.

*Haley:* Okay.

*Subject #4:* **Yes, I see other people.**
*E Film:* **You see other people. And you can talk, and you can hear. Tell me, can you keep your eyes open?**
*Subject #4:* **Yes.**
*E Film:* **You really can? You know I have the greatest doubts about that. I really have. They're closing. (She blinks.) All the way. And staying shut. (Her eyes remain closed.) That's right.**

*Erickson:* You saw, about three sentences before, her eyeballs turn up. Then she had to open her eyes, and when she finally closed them she again turned the eyeballs up. That's why you tell a subject to close your eyes and look at the top of your head, and get the eyes in the sleeping position.

*E Film:* **Really enjoy sleeping deeply and peacefully and bear in mind that in the future for dental or medical purposes you can go into a trance very easily and very comfortably. For any legitimate purpose. And you know that, don't you?**
*Subject #4:* **Yes.**

*Erickson:* The lifting of her hand was cut out. Everything I said about the lifting of her hand. I don't recall what it was.

*E Film:* **And now your broken leg is healed. And now take a deep breath and feel wide awake and refreshed and energetic. (She opens her eyes.)**

*Erickson:* There was a suggestion about the passage of time that was cut out. I have forgotten if I changed the date from October to March or whatever it was. She did very well. I think I asked if there was so much snow last Christmas. And that was the year that Philadelphia had that horrible blizzard. Alright.

*E Film:* **By the way, what is your name?**
*Subject#4:* **Mary.**
*E Film:* **What?**
*Subject: Mary.*
*E Film:* **Do you always keep your hand up in the air like that?**
*Subject #4:* **No, not usually.**
*E Film:* **Why are you keeping it up there now?**
*Subject #4:* **I don't know. (laughs)**
*E Film:* **You don't know. You know, women are the strangest creatures**

**there are. They are delightful. You know, half of my ancestors are women. And I'm so glad of it. What would I do without them? Do you think you can keep your hand up there?**

*Haley:* Now why did that hand stay up after you awakened her?

*Erickson:* Because I lifted her hand up out of context with something else I was doing. So the lifting of the hand might have been—suppose you take this with your left hand and I lift your right. Your attention is on taking this, so this would be out of context with your right hand. Your right hand will remain up. Your left hand would be free to move naturally.

*E Film:* **Did you ever see a woman successfully disputed before? (Laughter)**

*Subject #4:* **No.**

*E Film:* **Would you like to see her disputed successfully again? Try keeping your eyes open.**

*Haley:* Milton, why do you make such a thing about females in this one?

*Erickson:* Well, women range from masculine to very feminine. And this girl was very feminine in her behavior. Therefore, I emphasize it.

*E Film:* **Really try. Try harder. You can do better than that, try harder. Try to keep them from staying closed. (She closes her eyes.) That's right.**

*Erickson:* I told the cameraman repeatedly, "Don't focus on me. It's the subject that's important. Only my words." But you see he played up me much more than he should have, and he omitted really important things, and the film was chopped in that same way.

*E Film:* **You know, women are human beings too. Thank goodness for that. Now take a deep breath and wake up wide awake feeling rested and refreshed...**

*Haley:* Now why on earth do you say, "Women are human beings too?" It's things like this in this film that are puzzling.

*Erickson:* There was a chopping of the film cut there. Part of that is omitted.

*Haley:* Well, what was going on that this would be an appropriate statement for her, "Women are human beings too?"

*Erickson:* The film is not only chopped up, but it's spliced wrong. It didn't get the correct sequences.

*Haley:* With this last subject?

*Erickson:* Yes. The sequences are wrong. And I didn't mention that because not having a memory of the exact thing, I couldn't explain the transitions. I couldn't say anything of value about that, except to say the film was cut and spliced in the wrong way.

*Haley:* Okay.

*(It is typical of Erickson to reward subjects by giving some helpful suggestion to them. Sometimes subjects would indicate a problem, and Erickson would intervene therapeutically without the audience having any idea what he was doing. Erickson never stopped helping people, whether they asked explicitly for help or they simply showed him a problem. With demonstration hypnotic subjects, Erickson typically gave them suggestions that would be helpful to them, and he always did it in a way that the audience would not know the problem or how he was influencing that person. Sometimes his followers misunderstood his procedure. I recall a disciple demonstrating before a large audience, and he asked that the subject tell him a problem so he could help her with it. The woman was forced to reveal a problem to colleagues and strangers. Erickson would never work that way. He worked in indirect and private ways to reward his subjects for coming up and volunteering. When he influenced a subject in this private way, he was also helping someone who had not explicitly asked him to influence her to change.*

*Those of us who teach therapists must often restrain them from rushing about helping people who have not asked for help. In Erickson's case I was never concerned about that. Not only was he a benevolent and ethical man, but his judgment on when to influence people and when not to was sound. An additional factor that is sometimes not known is that he thought in a special way about communication in relationship to him. He assumed that if a volunteer subject expressed a problem to him, the subject was not merely reporting a problem but indicating a request for help with that problem. As Gregory Bateson put it, "Every message is both a report and a command." In these situations, Erickson received the indication of a problem as a command, or request, that he do something about it. He responded therapeutically, and maintained confidentiality by working in such a metaphoric way that only the subject knew what was happening. Often the subject only knew because of a later change.*

*One might assume that Erickson's response to questions about this last hypnotic subject indicate that something is being concealed. Rather than answer a question about why he emphasized female issues in this induction, he shifts to the ways the film was cut. He emphasizes femininity with this subject more than any other. When queried, he said, "Well, women range from masculine to very feminine. And this girl was very feminine in her behavior. Therefore I emphasized it." As a matter of fact, this woman did not seem feminine in her behavior, granting that is a subjective judgment. She wore a masculine suit and seemed less feminine than previous subjects. Even if she was very feminine in her behavior, it would seem odd that Erickson would emphasize that. A possible hypothesis is that Erickson thought, from the ways this woman expressed herself to him, she needed to feel and be more feminine. Therefore, he makes a large issue of how a man finds her so feminine. It is a way he often used his masculinity with female clients. Since he always concealed the problem, he would deny that his emphasis was helping this woman with a problem. After making a close relationship with the subject, by emphasizing femininity, he follows that by stepping back properly as he shows her his fondness for his wife.)*

*E Film: (continuing)* . . . **energetic, and wake up wide awake. (She opens her eyes.) And now I'm going to have the prettiest girl on the platform. Do you mind my saying that?**
*Subject #4:* **No.**
*E Film:* **Do you know why I say that?**
*Subject #4:* **Your wife?**
*E Film:* **It's my wife. And I've got good judgment.**

*Erickson:* Now how could she have reacted to that statement? And what they omitted there was I used my arm to direct the cameraman to take in the other subjects that the audience could pay attention to. The difference in this girl's response to "It's my wife." Because the other girls being in the movement situation made a response looking toward Betty. And this girl didn't. She and I were in total context. My wife wasn't in it. But for the others Betty was in it, and their heads moved. And I had indicated to the cameraman to include the subjects, but they omitted that.

*E Film:* **And thank you so much for your help.**

*(In the next part of the film Elizabeth Erickson demonstrates autohypnosis.)*

I will not attempt to detail what I believe Erickson was doing in this demonstration, but a few general comments are appropriate. Erickson conducted hundreds of demonstrations like this at seminars and medical meetings. In this one he had only a few minutes with each subject, and yet he behaved as casually as if he had hours. With each subject he demonstrated a different approach. Sometimes he was forceful and overwhelming, and sometimes gentle and encouraging. He would put a subject in charge at one moment, and within that framework paradoxically take charge himself. With all the subjects he demonstrated different kinds of involuntary behavior, usually using the lifting of a hand or an eye closure. He worked with direct suggestions and with indirect influence. Again and again he developed amnesia in various ways, which was his great specialty. His use of puns is not emphasized here but is obvious. He often pointed out how words had multiple meanings and could change meanings depending upon one's vocal emphasis. As an example, he could say, "You won't *know* that," in a way that meant, You won't "*no*" that, meaning it will not be negated. His phrasing is typically calculated, as when he says, "You'll do that, will you not?" As he taught, when told they will do something, some subjects think, "I will not." They cannot resist in that manner if Erickson has already taken the negative away from them. This induction illustrates the complexities of paradox in hypnotic inductions as well as the multilevels of message that constantly occur.

I think it is interesting that Erickson's comments on why he did what he did are so often interpersonal and contextual in this discussion. That is, he often points out that he is communicating to the social context while ostensibly talking with the subject. Some Erickson followers believe he was not interpersonal in his views but focused upon the individual, and that I exaggerated his interpersonal focus. Yet here he often comments that his suggestions were done for the other volunteers, or for the audience, as well as for the subject, perhaps knowing that was my interest. Similarly, his comments were directed toward analyzing the film but also were appropriate for his son who was in the room and for Madeleine Richeport and her interests.

Observing this demonstration, one would never know that Erickson was so ill that day that he had difficulty functioning and could hardly remember what he had done. If he was so skillful when ill, one can only imagine how he conducted such a demonstration when he was well. Having seen a few of those, I can only regret that he was not filmed more often.

# A Cognitive Contextual Theory and Classification of Milton H. Erickson's Hypnotherapeutic Techniques

## Akira Otani, Ed.D.

*One of the growing trends in contemporary Ericksonian approaches is the emphasis on contexts to create therapeutic change. While the term frequently appears in Ericksonian literature, little has been written about the fundamental nature of context on the basis of available scientific facts. This article will accomplish the following two goals: (1) review major characteristics of context from a cognitive psychological perspective, and (2) classify 29 representative hypnotherapeutic techniques of Erickson using a contextual taxonomy. As a heuristic concept, context has broad clinical and research applications to Ericksonian hypnosis and therapy.*

The hypnotherapeutic innovations of Milton H. Erickson (e.g., Erickson & Rossi, 1979, 1981; Erickson, Rossi, & Rossi, 1976; Haley, 1973, 1985; Rossi, 1980; Zeig, 1980) have gained wide recognition and acceptance among professionals in recent years. As the popularity and interest in Erickson's work continue to grow, his contributions need be examined and understood in terms of established scientific paradigms. To achieve this objective, several writers have proposed theoretical models to explain his therapy. For example, Rossi (1986, 1988) formulated a psychobiological theory of Ericksonian therapeutic hypnosis. Similarly, Matthews (1985) and Sherman (1988) delineated, independently, social psychological and cybernetic models to account for the mechanisms underlying Erickson's therapy. These works are based on empirical and theoretical foundations in psychology, biology, and systems theory.

The author gratefully acknowledges the conceptual works of B. J. Baars for contemporary views of contexts. Any inaccuracies about their description in this article are, however, the author's responsibility. Correspondence regarding this article should be addressed to: Akira Otani, Counseling Center, Shoemaker Hall, University of Maryland, College Park, MD 20742-8111.

In addition to these theoretical endeavors, noted clinicians (e.g., Haley, 1973; Lankton & Lankton, 1983; Watzlawick, Weakland, & Fisch, 1974; Zeig & Geary, 1990) elucidated principles and techniques permeating Erickson's hypnotherapy. Although these authors posit divergent views of change mechanisms and therapeutic techniques underlying Erickson's teachings (e.g., ordeal, metaphor, reframing), they concur that *successful therapy must identify, access, and alter the context in which maladaptive behavior occurs.* This assertion stands in direct contrast to the traditional intrapsychic premise that holds insight to be an integral part of therapy. As clinical reports of Erickson and others (Haley, 1973; Rossi, 1980; Watzlawick et al., 1974) suggest, this intrapsychic assumption may not be necessarily correct; instead, behavior change frequently seems to follow appropriate contextual modification. Erickson (e.g., Erickson & Rossi, 1979) himself acknowledged this therapeutic principle and stressed altering the patient's "frame of reference" in clinical hypnotherapy.

On the basis of this conceptual schema, O'Hanlon and Wilk (1987) elaborated on specific contextual shifting strategies from a clinical epistemological point of view. Like their predecessors, Bateson (1979) and Watzlawick et al. (1974), O'Hanlon and Wilk regarded human problems as being defined by contexts, and thus argued for contextual manipulation for therapeutic gain. Following this line of logic, they introduced three distinct classes of contextual strategies: contextual intervention, recontextualization, and decontextualization. A similar attempt was made by Hayes and Melancon (1989). Unusual to their theoretical orientation, these authors argued from a traditional behavior analytic position that psychological disturbance consists in emotional avoidance of aversive response vis-à-vis external stimuli. This mechanism presumably is maintained by what they call the "context of literalty," which *erroneously* convinces the patient to link emotional arousal with the context in which it occurs. For example, a snake phobic typically believes that he or she is afraid of snakes, and thus avoids any situation where snakes may be present (context). What the phobic fails to realize is that it is the internal fear response (arousal), *not* the situation, that is truly noxious to him or her. This conceptual distinction of context and arousal should allow, according to Hayes and Melancon, differential assessment and modification of the maladaptive response by way of contextual examinations. They proposed specific clinical strategies for treatment, including paradoxes, metaphors, and confusion.

Although these authors deserve praise for recognizing and assimilating contextual roles in human change process, they neither defined context explicitly nor examined various functional properties of context. As the reader will learn in the next sections of this article, recent advances in experimental cognitive psychology illuminate the role of contexts in both conscious and unconscious information processing. In addition, context proves to be a useful concept to classify Erickson's hypnotherapeutic techniques. This article has two principal goals: (1) to review relevant characteristics of context on the basis of available cognitive psychological research findings, and (2) to categorize 29 major hypnotherapeutic techniques of Erickson according to a parsimonious contextual framework. These attempts are believed to foster better understanding of Erickson's clinical strategies with reference to current empirical findings.

## Characteristics of Context: Theoretical and Empirical Perspective

Although the term context appears frequently in Ericksonian clinical literature, little has been written about its characteristics and functions, particularly in relation to human cognition. Because context has a profound impact upon memory, perception, comprehension, learning, and emotion, it has strong relevance to hypnotic induction and therapy.

### Definition of Context and Its Therapeutic Implication

Cognitive psychology (Baars, 1989; Bransford & Johnson, 1972) defines context as an internal influence that mediates information processing without itself being consciously recognized by the individual. This definition points out that contexts are essential facets for the access, retrieval, and comprehension of information. Without them, even the simplest data cannot be understood sufficiently (see below for further discussion). Moreover, contexts are *unconscious, internal influences* rather than external factors, such as situational constraints or circumstances. Thus the individual's private phenomena—for example, personality styles and values— can become powerful contexts. In this regard, the cognitive psychological definition of context resembles such concepts as frame of reference, mental set, and psychological perspective (Baars, 1989).

Given this definition of contexts, it is small wonder that contemporary theorists (Mahoney, 1985; Mahoney & Lyddon, 1988) have come to view context as a central facet in the change process. According to these authors, behavior change can result from (1) modification of problematic thought and/or affect (e.g., cognitive restructuring, focused experiential therapy [Greenberg & Safran, 1989]) or (2) the systemic transformation of problem-related contexts (Watzlawick et al., 1974). In psychotherapy literature, the former model of change process is denoted as first-order change, while the latter as second-order change. These change paradigms characterize "change without change" (first-order change) and "change of change" (second-order change), respectively, from a philosophical standpoint (Lyddon, 1990). As Erickson (1948) contended more than 40 years ago, the adaptation of a new frame of reference was a cardinal aspect of effective hypnotic psychotherapy. One can argue, therefore, that the idea of second-order change was rooted in Erickson's work (Zeig & Geary, 1990).

## Characteristics of Contexts

Research evidence (Baars, 1989; Wapner, 1986; Watkins, 1990) shows that contexts have the following important characteristics pertinent to hypnosis and hypnotic therapy.

*Facilitation of Meaning Comprehension*

One of the essential features of contexts is to clarify the meanings of information for easy and accurate understanding. Studies indicate that contexts assign relevant "rules" to information for decoding its message. Without contexts, these rules will not be available, and any information, even a simple message, becomes unintelligible. Bransford and Johnson (1972) demonstrated this principle experimentally by presenting the subjects with a series of paragraphs, each describing a specific situation or task, such as "washing clothes." These researchers found that the subjects who had the contextual knowledge showed significantly better comprehension of the material than those who did not. In a later study, Winograd and Rivers-Bulkeley (1977) showed that contexts also mediate the individual's ability to recognize faces. These findings strongly suggest that contexts serve a pivotal function in enhancing semantic as well as perceptual information comprehension.

Understandably, this contextual property has been adopted in trance induction and hypnotherapeutic procedures to augment the effects of suggestion. Consider, for instance, an arm-levitation suggestion: "Your hand will move up *as if it has a helium balloon attached to it.*" In this example, the directive for hand levitation is followed by an italicized metaphor to provide a vivid context appropriate to the suggestion. The introduction of this context not only helps to clarify the intended suggestion, but it also promotes the subject's desired hypnotic response to the directive. Because of this effect, metaphors and analogies are powerful contextual tools to reinforce hypnotic suggestion. This issue will be addressed further in the next section with respect to its clinical applicability (i.e., "Context Formation").

*Alteration of Meaning*

In addition to clarifying and facilitating comprehension of meaning, contexts can alter the perceived meaning of an event or behavior. Gregory Bateson, a friend and colleague of Erickson, summarized succinctly the relationship between contexts and meaning as follows: "'Context' is linked to another undefined notion called 'meaning.' Without context, words and actions have no meaning at all. . .It is the *context* that fixes the meaning" (Bateson, 1979, p. 15; emphasis in original).

From a cognitive psychological perspective, Tversky and Kahneman (1981) used mathematical models to elucidate how alterations of contexts could lead to a profound change in judgment and decision making. To illustrate, most Americans today would consider $9.99 for a 16-ounce T-bone steak dinner "inexpensive," and yet the same price, $9.99, for a regular hamburger would be "too expensive." Clearly, as Tversky and Kahneman pointed out, the monetary judgment is *not* determined by the actual cost of the meal ($9.99), but by its *relative value* to the purchase (steak versus hamburger). This example corroborates the observation that contexts influence the perceived meaning of an event or behavior by transforming its figure–ground relationship to the whole.

The best-known clinical application of this contextual principle is reframing. According to Watzlawick et al. (1974), reframing means "to change the conceptual and/or emotional setting or viewpoint in relation to which a situation is experienced and place it in another frame which fits the 'facts' of the same concrete situation equally well or even better, and thereby changes its entire meaning" (p. 95).

This definition underscores the contextual role in reframing. Empirical evidence (Conoley & Garber, 1985; Kolko & Milan, 1983; Schnarch, 1989) indicates that reframing, particularly positive reframing of negative events, is effective for a wide range of problems, including depression, marital conflict, sexual dysfunction, and delinquent behavior.

*Generation of Ambiguity and Confusion*

Although an explicit context helps to clarify meaning and to facilitate the comprehension of information, the presence of multiple contexts occasionally can create ambiguity and confusion. This phenomenon is especially noticeable when two or more contexts are "at odds" with one another. For example, the sentence, "John has been hypnotized many times, but he has never experienced a trance," makes little sense because the context elicited by the first sentence ("being hypnotized many times") is incompatible with that implied by the second statement ("never having experienced a trance"). Studies on reading comprehension by Carpenter and Just (Carpenter & Just, 1989; Just & Carpenter, 1980) suggest that the use of an elaborate grammatical structure, polysemous or multimeaning words, and technical jargon slows down cognitive information processing. One plausible interpretation of this finding is that these linguistic elements may engender multiple contexts and interfere with ordinary cognitive processes, thereby causing confusion in the subject.

This contextual view renders theoretical as well as empirical support for Erickson's confusion technique (Erickson, 1964). Content analysis of confusion suggestions reveals that Erickson produced hypnotic confusion by way of skillful manipulation of incongruous contexts using various word plays, non sequiturs, interruptions, puns and riddles, and difficult words (Otani, 1989a). This is illustrated in the following remark of Erickson to a patient: "I wonder how you feel about not being able to *write here* now in the office?" (Haley, 1985, p. 205). Notice that the italicized phrase is ambiguous because of its dual context representation (*"write* here" versus *"right* here"). Besides, while this directive was suggested to the patient, she was instructed to hold a pencil in her *left* hand, her non*writing* hand, at the same time. As this example illustrates, the therapeutic adaptation of multiple contexts can intensify the effects of confusion. Drawing on this point, Lankton and Lankton (1989) speculated that a hypnotic subject may initiate a five-stage search-evaluation process called enchantment as he or she experiences contextually induced confusion. According to their formulation, therapeutic change occurs when the patient successfully reduces the incongruity between the current, anomalous context and a new, adaptive context. This conceptualization is intriguing and warrants empirical validation.

*Priming Effect*

Another intriguing feature of contexts is the priming effect. In cognitive psychology, priming refers to the influence of prior cues on subsequent resembling responses. Baars (1989) lists many everyday phenomena that occur as a result of priming effects. One such example concerns asking people to repeat the word poke (priming), and then asking the question: "What do you call the white of an egg?" Because of the semantic priming created by the word poke, most people respond with the answer "yolk." In a laboratory situation, Motley and Baars (1976) showed earlier that the subjects would mispronounce "rage weight" as "wage rate," following a priming with a phrase "salary scale." Experimental cognitive psychology literature is replete with studies like this one, demonstrating different priming effects on human cognition (see Baars, 1989; Sherman, 1988). On the basis of available experimental data, Baars (1988, 1989) argued that semantic and perceptual stimuli are capable of forming contexts, and they will shape various facets of conscious experience by way of the priming mechanism.

From the Ericksonian perspective, the concept of priming has been referred to as seeding. According to Zeig (1990), the seeding strategy is "a logical outgrowth of the 'utilization' approach championed by Erickson" (p. 233). Although the utilization approach has broader clinical implications in light of contemporary contextual theory, Erickson was fully cognizant of the pivotal function of priming when he discussed a hypnotic "yes set" in trance induction (Erickson, 1965/1983). "The more times you get patients to say, 'Yes, yes, yes, yes, yes,'" emphasized Erickson, "the more adequately you have started them on this matter of hypnosis" (p. 238). In clinical induction of hypnosis, Erickson would typically make truism statements, thus priming a yes set or seeding an idea to respond affirmatively to his remarks. Once this context was established, the patient's continued compliance with other hypnotic suggestion was warranted. It was Erickson's genius that enabled him to create such therapeutic contexts with a wide range of individuals, even the most resistant patients.

*State of Absorption*

When an individual's conscious awareness is immersed in an immediately available context, he or she is said to be in a state of absorption (Baars, 1989). Absorption states have many traits that characterize hypnotic trance, including various cognitive and perceptual changes, such as time distortion, narrowed attention, heightened involvement in imagination and fantasy, and lowered distractibility. Because of this evidence, some theorists, most notably Tellegen and Atkinson (1974), maintained that absorption was an essential component of hypnotic susceptibility. A common yet most compelling example of contextual dominance, or absorption, is seen in a child who is watching his or her favorite cartoons on a Saturday morning. During the show, the most active child is preoccupied, obviously unaware of anything but the cartoon characters that predominate his or her conscious experience. The child literally does not hear the parents, feel thirst or hunger, or recognize the passage of time. From the hypnotic perspective, the child is in trance to the degree to which he or she is absorbed in the TV show.

Erickson's view of trance corroborates this contextual interpretation of hypnotic phenomena. He regarded fixation of attention and its intentional focusing on internal cognitive cues as the essence of trance induction. For instance, he stated: "A trusted operator can progressively, persuasively, and repetitiously suggest tiredness, relaxation, eye closure, *loss of interest in externalities and an increased absorbing interest in inner experiential process*, until the subject can function with increasing adequacy at the level of unconscious awareness" (Erickson, 1970, p. 995; emphasis added).

As this quote suggests, Erickson considered hypnotic induction as consisting of two basis principles: (1) creating a context using the patient's own internal response (e.g., memory, image, sensation), and (2) assisting the patient to become absorbed in that context. This premise appears to be empirically tenable in view of macrodynamic analysis of Erickson's trance induction transcripts (Otani, 1989b).

To summarize, contexts have five important characteristics: (1) facilitation of meaning comprehension, (2) alternation of meaning, (3) generation of confusion and ambiguity, (4) priming effect, and (5) elicitation of absorption states. Each of these properties has direct relevance to clinical hypnosis and accounts well for Erickson's approach to hypnotherapy.

# Classification of Erickson's Techniques by Contextual Schemata

The foregoing discussion clarifies the roles of contexts in information processing and their relevance to Erickson's approach to hypnosis. Although it is not feasible to fit all of Erickson's techniques into a unified contextual system, many of them fall into one of six categories. These categories are (1) context formation, (2) context utilization, (3) context fusion, (4) context violation, (5) context destruction, and (6) context alteration. Table 1 is a summary of the contextual classification of Erickson's major hypnotic techniques.

---

Table 1
Contextual Schemata and Hypnotherapeutic Techniques

---

1. *Context formation:*    Form and develop clinically meaningful contexts.
    Metaphors, analogies, therapeutic tales
    Indirect associative focusing
    Double binds
    Truisms
    The yes set
    Age regression
    Sensory-perceptual alterations

2. *Context utilization:*    Utilize the existing contexts of the patient.
    The utilization approach
    Implication
    The implied directive

3. *Context fusion:*    Incorporate two or more compatible contexts simultaneously.
    Two-level communication
    The interspersal technique
    Compound and contingent suggestion
    Structured amnesia

4. *Context violation:*    Confound the existing contexts with incompatible competing contexts.
    The confusion technique
    Apposition of opposites
    Cognitive overload
    Interruption, hesitation, mispronunciation

5. *Context destruction:*  Destroy the existing contexts of the patient.
                           Shock, surprise

6. *Context alteration:*   Shift the dysfunctional contexts of the patient
                           into positive.
                           Reframing
                           Symptom prescription
                           Therapeutic ordeal
                           Spatial rearrangement

## Context Formation

Techniques in this category are designed to *form and develop clinically meaningful contexts. Metaphors, analogies,* and *therapeutic tales* provide the patient with new contextual frameworks that will facilitate problem assessment and resolution. Once established, these contexts can help to accelerate the patient's comprehension of the therapeutic message. *Indirect associative* focusing generates, through verbal association, a personal context that is relevant to the patient. For instance, Erickson would talk about *his* mother and father in order to have the patient discuss his or her own parents "spontaneously." Clearly, as this example illuminates, contexts play an important role in indirect associative focusing. *Double binds* also establish contexts in the form of a no-lose inquiry. For example, a double-bind question, "Are you going to experience a light or medium trance?," commits a hypnotic subject to a context of trance experience regardless of the answer selected. From the contextual point of view, therefore, therapeutic double binds consist in the process of contextual commitment through illusory choice. *Truisms* and *the yes set* help to create and consolidate contexts as well. Truisms refer to factual, unrefutable statements designed to enhance the patient's compliance. The skillful use of truisms in trance induction can quickly establish a hypnotic yes set (Erickson & Rossi, 1979). These techniques define contexts in a hypnotic process and compel the patient to affirm them as a valid hypnotic experience.

Of all hypnotherapeutic techniques reported by Erickson, *age regression* and *sensory-perceptual alterations* (e.g., hallucination, analgesia) rely most heavily on the mechanism of context formation. To evoke these hypnotic phenomena, Erickson (see Erickson & Rossi, 1979, 1989) would build elaborate experiential and perceptual contexts to fit the patient in advance through careful indirect suggestion. Only within the boundaries of these predetermined contexts would appropriate age-regressed behavior and hypnotic blindness/deafness emerge. Formation of relevant contexts was evidently central to Erickson's approach to hypnosis.

A case in point is Erickson's use of metaphorical communication with a 71-year-old patient suffering from phantom limb pain in an amputated arm (Haley, 1985). This patient had worked as a carpenter laying floors for 27 years prior to the accident that claimed his arm. During the initial interview, the patient mentioned his two brothers. Erickson learned about one of them, but not about the other. On the basis of this partial knowledge of his background information, Erickson developed a metaphor that would match the patient's psychological and historical contexts. He added:

> If I really wanted to find out more about his family background, I might start talking about driving in the desert. I would describe driving along the road and rounding a high point rising from the desert floor. Suddenly rounding that high point, I would see a rather lonesome ironwood tree. One of the branches had been broken, probably by the wind smashing around that high point. I would use the image of "ironwood" because of that man's work history. An ironwood tree with a broken branch (Haley, 1973, pp. 30–31).

Note how Erickson incorporated in this verbalization the essential information of the patient and organized it into a context that was meaningful and familiar to him. Given the highly metaphorical nature of Erickson's communication, the patient's response would be equally symbolic and unconscious in nature, which would be comprehensible only in that context. Nevertheless, Erickson collected sufficient facts about the patient to relieve him of the pain. This vignette demonstrates a clinical application of contextual formation strategy to diagnosis.

## Context Utilization

Erickson actively *utilized the patient's contexts* to yield hypnotic results. This *utilization approach* is a hallmark of Erickson's therapy and hypnotic trance induction. In principle, hypnotic utilization incorporates "some important aspect of [the patient's] own personality and behavior" (Erickson & Rossi, 1979, p. 53) as part of trance induction and the therapy process. Erickson's trance induction approach based on the vivification of past successful hypnotic experience is an application of this principle. It utilizes the patient's experiential memory to re-create trance. According to Erickson and Rossi (1979), the six sources of utilization are (1) the patient's manifest behavior, (2) inner resources, (3) resistances, (4) negative affects and confusion, (5) symptoms, and (6) emergency situations. In light of the contextual theory, the first five attributes are different expressions of the individual's idiosyncratic contexts, whereas the last one is a contributor to the formation of such contexts. Hence contextual access and mobilization account for Erickson's utilization approach.

*Implication* and *the implied directive* also utilize the patient's existing contexts. These techniques convey hypnotic directives through subtle verbal and/or nonverbal cues, such as tonal inflections, verbal associations, and body language. Macrodynamic analysis of Erickson's trance induction process reveals that these techniques characteristically succeed truisms and indirect associative focusing forms of suggestion. As mentioned earlier in this article, these indirect suggestions can swiftly form contexts when implemented for trance induction (Otani, 1989b). Once the contexts are available, the implication strategies then operate directly on these contexts to structure their meaning. As a result, they initiate inner search and unconscious response in the patient (Erickson & Rossi, 1979).

A brilliant example of context utilization is depicted in the case of Harold (Haley, 1973, pp. 120–148), who consulted Erickson for "character revision." When he first came to Erickson's office, Harold was "unshaven and unwashed" and said, "I ain't nothing but a damn dumb no-good moron, but I ain't never done anything wrong. . .I just hurt all over and, Mister, I can't stand it no more" (p. 120). To this dramatic plea for help, Erickson responded:

> "Listen you, listen to me. *You are nothing but a miserable moron.* You know how to work, you want help. *You don't know nothing* about doctoring. I do. You sit down *in that there chair* and you let me go to work." *I phrased that statement deliberately in keeping with his mood and in a fashion calculated to arrest and fixate his attention.* When he sat down, bewildered, he was virtually in a light trance. (p. 121; emphasis added)

Note that Erickson quickly acknowledged and utilized the patient's contextual framework by emulating Harold's nongrammatical speech pattern and helplessness in his reply. This contextual utilization evoked a spontaneous trance in the patient, verifying a solid rapport between Erickson and Harold. As Haley (1973) points out, accurate modeling of a patient's immediate context, albeit its pathological nature, communicates the therapist's respect for and acceptance of the patient. This case study of Harold convincingly demonstrates this principle.

## Context Fusion

This term refers to *the simultaneous engagement of two or more compatible contexts* with the patient. *Two-level communication* (Erickson & Rossi, 1976) is an exemplary technique of context fusion. An illustrative two-level communication is a hypnotist's remark to a volunteer subject, "Are you ready (pause) *to go into a trance?*" The initial phrase ("Are you ready") taps into a motivational context of the subject, followed by a directive (*"to go into a trance"*) engaging directly into the trance induction context. The two statements are merged into one meaningful sentence, each activating different contextual responses. This dual context view of two-level communication parallels Erickson's theoretical position that the first part of the sentence is addressed to the conscious mind, while the suggestion component is addressed to the unconscious (Erickson & Rossi, 1979).

An extension of two-level communication is the *interspersal technique.* This elaborate form of context fusion strategy interpolates multiple indirect suggestions into a cohesive text. In the well-known case of Joe, Erickson (1966) successfully maneuvered three contexts (trance induction, pain control, and illness coping) of a terminally ill patient, a florist, through suggestions interspersed in a tale of a tomato plant. Context fusion is also the foundation of the *compound* and *contingent* forms of suggestion. The former arranges two (or more) suggestions serially, whereas the latter makes one suggestion contingent upon another. The juxtaposition of these suggestions results in contextual mixture. The desired hypnotic response emerges consequently.

An ingenious variation of context fusion is Erickson's indirect approach to *structured amnesia* (Erickson & Rossi, 1979, p. 122). Erickson would typically begin hypnotic induction with a casual conversation, thus establishing a context in the patient's awakened state. He would then introduce a second context in which trance occurs. At the termination of the trance work, he would swiftly "switch back" to the original conversation (the first context) or initiate a new topic to form a third context. The context associated with the trance experience is thus interpolated between the two contexts. As a result, it will be excluded from conscious awareness, producing amnesia for the trance experience in the patient.

## Context Violation

In the case of context violation, the patient's *currently operational context is confounded by competing contexts.* Clinical consequences of such assault on a prevailing context ranges from cognitive-perceptual disorientation to momentary mental absorption. A prime example of context violation is the *confusion technique* (Erickson, 1964). By means of various word plays and non sequiturs designed for contextual violation, Erickson would confuse and restructure the patient's mental set to gain hypnotic responses from the patient. This confusion-restructuring sequence is the essence of Erickson's confusion technique (Otani, 1989a). To a lesser degree, contextual disturbance is involved in the forms of indirect suggestion known as *apposition of opposites* and *cognitive overloading*. Apposition of opposites is a form of suggestion consisting of two opposing directives, such as "As one hand gets *lighter*, the other hand starts feeling *heavy*." Cognitive overloading, in contrast, comprises multiple suggestions for specific tasks as illustrated in this suggestion: "You can *breathe* comfortably and *focus* your attention on my voice. As you *continue paying* attention to my voice, let the trance *deepen* and you can *feel* more relaxed." Although these two strategies are not as intense as the confusion technique in their effect, their main goal is the temporary halting and disorganization of the patient's ordinary contexts.

Other effective methods of contextual violation include *interruption, hesitation,* and *mispronunciation*. These techniques can seriously violate contexts currently upheld by the patient, causing discomfort and an intense need for closure (i.e., Zeigarnik effect). In clinical situations, Erickson would purposely pause in the middle of suggestions or err on certain words and phrases, so that the patient would be forced to complete the contexts by filling in or correcting Erickson's suggestion.

One area of clinical applications for context violation is resistance management. See the following excerpt in which Erickson utilized confusion to displace the patient's resistance. The patient, a school teacher, experienced severe verbal blocking during the history taking.

> I asked [the patient] to hold [the pencil] in her *left* hand. She looked at me with some question and held it in her *left* hand. I said, "Of course, you are *right* handed; but after you've held it in your *left* hand, I want you to hold it in your *writing* hand. You really can't *write* yet, can you? Not until you get home. I wonder how you feel about not being able to *write* here now in the office? Do you think you'll be glad to be able to *write* at home for me?" And she started talking. (Haley, 1985, p. 205; emphasis added)

Here, Erickson first violated the patient's resistance-related context by having her hold the pencil in the nondominant "wrong" hand. He then restructured the contextual framework by introducing the "left–right–write" verbal confusion. This intervention succeeded in reversing the resistance. Future investigation is awaited to analyze other resistance management techniques of Erickson on the basis of the contextual theory.

## Context Destruction

Erickson would sometimes *deliberately destroy the patient's contexts*, especially if they were "rigid" or fixed on pathological patterns. *"The most important thing in therapy,"* contended Erickson (Erickson & Rossi, 1979, p. 343), *"is to break up the patient's rigid and limiting mental sets"* (emphasis original). To destroy contexts, Erickson would employ *shock* and *surprise* in trance induction and hypnotherapy work. Commenting on these strategies, Erickson and Rossi (1979) wrote:

> A shock surprises patients' habitual mental frameworks so their usual conscious sets are depotentiated and there is a momentary gap in their awareness, which can then be filled with an appropriate suggestion. . . . The shock opens the possibility of a creative moment during which the patient's unconscious is engaged in an inner search for an answer or conception that can reestablish psychic equilibrium.

Undoubtedly, Erickson's rationale for the use of shock and surprise was to shatter the patient's maladaptive contexts. Clinical applications of shock and surprise include trance induction with a highly resistant subject (Erickson, 1964) and therapy for patients suffering from long-standing self-defeating behavior (Rossi, 1973).

Erickson and Rossi's clinical formulation of therapeutic shock and surprise has empirical and theoretical support as well. Based on the review of recent work by Underwood (1982) and Grossberg (1982), Baars (1988) argued, "Surprise often seems to be accompanied by a moment of conscious 'emptiness,' . . . [it] may have the function of *resetting consciousness . . . it allows conscious processes to start anew, uninhibited by previous contents"* (pp. 277–278; emphasis added). This observation in contemporary cognitive psychology corroborates Erickson's ingenuity in the clinical use of shock and surprise. Carefully planned and administered destruction of patients' self-limiting contexts can lead to change in behavior and cognition.

## Context Alteration

Hypnotic techniques in this category *shift the patient's dysfunctional context* to achieve therapeutic results. An exemplary method of contextual alteration is *reframing*. It transforms the patient's negative interpretation of events or behavior into positive by changing the context in which they occur. Erickson himself (Erickson & Rossi, 1989, p. 77) explicated the objective of reframing by stating, "You don't alter the original experience; you alter the *perception* of it, and that becomes the memory of the perception" (emphasis original). Simple in definition, reframing can be a powerful strategy with a wide range of clinical applicability in such areas as habit control, symptom modification, and posttraumatic stress management (Erickson & Rossi, 1989; Watzlawick et al., 1974).

Context alteration can also explain the plausible mechanisms underlying *symptom prescription* and *therapeutic ordeal.* As mentioned in the previous section, contextual shifting changes the meaning of an event or behavior. Consequently, when recurring symptoms (e.g., obsessive checking) or ordeals (e.g., polishing shoes when one cannot sleep at night) are assigned to the patient as volitional acts or as indispensable therapeutic tasks to be exercised, they paradoxically can reshape the patient's attitude toward the "uncontrollable" behavior. This contextual change eventually leads to the correction of the manifest problem.

When working with couples and families, Erickson frequently employed *spatial rearrangement* to alter contexts that would undermine individuals' autonomy. He would typically ask spouses or family members to switch seats during a session. As they traded seats, Erickson would instruct them to examine the reality from the other members' frames of reference and to appreciate the different points of view (Haley, 1985). This nonverbal context alteration procedure can help patients to understand individual differences and resolve conflicts.

In summation, 29 representative hypnotherapeutic techniques of Erickson were classified according to a taxonomy based on six contextual functions: (1) context formation, (2) context utilization, (3) context fusion, (4) context violation, (5) context destruction, and (6) context alteration. The six categories provide a parsimonious framework to conceptualize Erickson's hypnotic strategies. Because contexts are well studied in cognitive psychology, the proposed contextual theory allows scientific assessment and refinement.

## Conclusion

Context is a central concept in modern cognitive psychology. It affects information processing, meaning formation, problem solving, and conscious states. This article represents an ambitious attempt to delineate Erickson's contributions from the emerging contextual perspective. It summarizes relevant empirical findings in the field of experimental cognitive psychology and classifies selected hypnotherapeutic techniques of Erickson according to a taxonomy while discussing their clinical implications. Given the demonstrated complexity of Erickson's hypnotherapeutic strategies, any classification effort faces an onerous challenge. Nevertheless, continued efforts are urged to gain more systematic knowledge about his contributions to clinical hypnosis and therapy.

# References

Baars, B. J. (1988). Momentary forgetting as a "resetting" of a conscious global workspace due to competition between incompatible contexts. In M. J. Horowitz (Ed.), *Psychodynamics and cognition* (pp. 269–293). Chicago: University of Chicago Press.

Baars, B. J. (1989). *A cognitive theory of consciousness.* New York: Cambridge University Press.

Bateson, G. (1979). *Mind and nature: A necessary unity.* New York: Dutton.

Bransford, J. D., & Johnson, M. K. (1972). Contextual prerequisites for understanding: Some investigations of comprehension and recall. *Journal of Verbal Learning and Learning Behavior, 11,* 717–726.

Carpenter, P. A., & Just, M. A. (1989). The role of working memory in language comprehension. In D. Klahr & K. Kotovsky (Eds.), *Complex information processing: The impact of Herbert S. Simon* (pp. 31–68). Hillsdale, N.J.: Erlbaum.

Conoley, C. W., & Garber, R. A. (1985). Effects of reframing and self-control directives on loneliness, depression, and controllability. *Journal of Counseling Psychology, 32,* 139–142.

Erickson, M. H. (1948). Hypnotic psychotherapy. *Medical Clinics of North America,* May, 571–583.

Erickson, M. H. (1964). The confusion technique in hypnosis. *American Journal of Clinical Hypnosis, 6,* 183–207.

Erickson, M. H. (1965/1983). An introduction to the study and the application of hypnosis in pain control. In E. L. Rossi, M. O. Ryan, & F. A. Sharp (Eds.), *The seminars, workshops, and lectures of Milton H. Erickson: Vol. 1: Healing in hypnosis* (pp. 217–277). New York: Irvington.

Erickson, M. H. (1966). The interspersal technique for symptom correction and pain control. *American Journal of Clinical Hypnosis, 8,* 198–209.

Erickson, M. H. (1970). Hypnosis. *Encyclopaedia Britannica* (14th ed), *11,* 995–997.

Erickson, M. H., & Rossi, E. L. (1976). Two-level communication and the microdynamics of trance and suggestion. *American Journal of Clinical Hypnosis, 18,* 153–171.

Erickson, M. H., & Rossi, E. L. (1979). *Hypnotherapy: An exploratory casebook.* New York: Irvington.

Erickson, M. H., & Rossi, E. L. (1981). *Experiencing hypnosis: Therapeutic approaches to altered states.* New York: Irvington.

Erickson, M. H., & Rossi, E. L. (1989). *The February man: Evolving consciousness and identity in hypnotherapy.* New York: Brunner/Mazel.

Erickson, M. H., Rossi, E. L., & Rossi, S. I. (1976). *Hypnotic realities: The induction of clinical hypnosis and forms of indirect suggestion.* New York: Irvington.

Greenberg, L. S., & Safran, J. D. (1989). Emotion in psychotherapy. *American Psychologist, 44,* 19–29.

Grossberg, S. (1982). *Studies of mind and brain.* Boston: Reidel.

Haley, J. (1973). *Uncommon therapy: The psychiatric techniques of Milton H. Erickson, M.D.* (Paperback edition). New York: Norton.

Haley, J. (Ed.). (1985). *Conversations with Milton H. Erickson, M.D.: Vol. 1: Changing individuals.* New York: Triangle Press.

Hayes, S. C., & Melancon, S. M. (1989). Comprehensive distancing, paradox, and the treatment of emotional avoidance. In L. M. Ascher (Ed.), *Therapeutic paradox* (pp. 184–218). New York: Guilford Press.

Just, M. A., & Carpenter, P. A. (1980). A theory of reading: From eye fixations to comprehension. *Psychological Review, 87,* 329–354.

Kolko, D., & Milan, M. (1983). Reframing and paradoxical instruction to overcome "resistance" in the treatment of delinquent youths: A multiple baseline analysis. *Journal of Consulting and Clinical Psychology, 51,* 655–660.

Lankton, C. M., & Lankton, S. R. (1989). *Tales of enchantment: Goal directed metaphors for adults and children in therapy.* New York: Brunner/Mazel.

Lankton, S. R., & Lankton, C. M. (1983). *The answer within: A clinical framework of Ericksonian hypnotherapy.* New York: Brunner/Mazel.

Lyddon, W. J. (1990). First- and second-order change: Implications for rationalist and constructivist cognitive therapies. *Journal of Counseling and Development, 69,* 122–127.

Mahoney, M. J. (1985). Psychotherapy and human change processes. In M. J. Mahoney & A. Freeman (Eds.), *Cognition and psychotherapy* (pp. 3–48). New York: Plenum.

Mahoney, M. J., & Lyddon, W. J. (1988). Recent developments in cognitive approaches to counseling and psychotherapy. *Counseling Psychologist, 16,* 190–234.

Matthews, W. J. (1985). A cybernetic model of Ericksonian hypnotherapy: One hand draws the other. In S. R. Lankton (Ed.), *Elements and dimensions of Ericksonian approach* (Ericksonian Monograph, vol. 1). New York: Brunner/Mazel.

Motley, M. T., & Baars, B. J. (1976). Semantic bias effects on the outcomes of verbal slips. *Cognition, 4,* 177–187.

O'Hanlon, B. W., & Wilk, J. (1987). *Shifting contexts: The generation of effective psychotherapy.* New York: Guilford Press.

Otani, A. (1989a). The confusion technique untangled: Its theoretical rationale and preliminary classification. *American Journal of Clinical Hypnosis, 31,* 164–172.

Otani, A. (1989b). An empirical investigation of Milton H. Erickson's approach to trance induction: A Markov chain analysis of two published cases. In S. R. Lankton (Ed.), *Ericksonian hypnosis: Application, preparation, and research* (Ericksonian Monograph, no. 5). New York: Brunner/Mazel.

Rossi, E. L. (1973). Psychological shocks and creative moments in psychotherapy. *American Journal of Clinical Hypnosis, 16,* 9–22.

Rossi, E. L. (Ed.). (1980). *The collected papers of Milton H. Erickson on hypnosis* (4 vols.). New York: Irvington.

Rossi, E. L. (1986). The state-dependent memory and learning theory of therapeutic hypnosis. In E. L. Rossi & M. O. Ryan (Eds.), *The seminars, workshops, and lectures of Milton H. Erickson: Vol. 3: Mind-body communication.* New York: Irvington.

Rossi, E. L. (1988). The psychobiology of mind-body healing: The vision and the state of the art. In J. K. Zeig & S. R. Lankton (Eds.), *Developing Ericksonian therapy: State of the art* (pp. 127–148). New York: Brunner/Mazel.

Schnarch, D. M. (1989). Use of inherent paradox in postmodern sexual-marital therapy. In L. M. Ascher (Ed.), *Therapeutic paradox* (pp. 219–254). New York: Guilford Press.

Sherman, S. J. (1988). Ericksonian psychotherapy and social psychology. In J. K. Zeig & S. R. Lankton (Eds.), *Developing Ericksonian therapy: State of the art* (pp. 59–90). New York: Brunner/Mazel.

Tellegen, A., & Atkinson, G. (1974). Openness to absorbing and self-altering experiences ("absorption"), a trait related to hypnotic susceptibility. *Journal of Abnormal Psychology, 83,* 268–277.

Tversky, A., & Kahneman, D. (1981). The framing of decisions and the psychology of choice. *Science, 21,* 453–458.

Underwood, G. (1982). Attention and awareness in cognitive and motor skills. In G. Underwood (Ed.), *Aspects of consciousness* (Vol. 3, pp. 111–146). New York: Academic Press.

Wapner, M. A. (1986). Interview with Michael A. Wapner. In B. J. Baars (Ed.), *The cognitive revolution in psychology* (pp. 315–336). New York: Guilford Press.

Watkins, M. J. (1990). Mediationism and the obfuscation of memory. *American Psychologist, 45,* 328–335.

Watzlawick, P., Weakland, J., & Fisch, R. (1974). *Change: Principles of problem formation and problem resolution.* New York: Norton.

Winograd, E., & Rivers-Bulkeley, N. T. (1977). Effects of changing context on remembering faces. *Journal of Experimental Psychology: Human Learning and Memory, 3,* 397–405.

Zeig, J. K. (1980). *A teaching seminar with Milton H. Erickson.* New York: Irvington.

Zeig, J. K. (1990). Seeding. In J. K. Zeig & S. G. Gilligan (Eds.), *Brief therapy: Myths, methods, and metaphors* (pp. 221–246). New York: Brunner/Mazel.

Zeig, J. K., & Geary, B. B. (1990). Seeds of strategic and interactional psychotherapies: Seminal contributions of Milton H. Erickson. *American Journal of Clinical Hypnosis, 33,* 105–112.

# A Multischema Model for Combining Ericksonian and Cognitive Therapy

## Jeffrey B. Feldman, Ph.D.

*The concept of cognitive schema previously presented as a conceptual bridge between Ericksonian hypnotherapy and cognitive therapy is developed into a multilevel construct. These levels include an individual's deep structures of stored experience, schemas about oneself, schemas about reality, and schemas for functioning in the world. While cognitive therapy typically focuses on conscious level schemas, and Ericksonian hypnotherapy bypasses conscious processes and accesses deep structures of stored experience, this multilevel schema model provides a conceptual outline for evaluating and intervening with a patient on multiple levels. In so doing, it takes into account complex interactions among the different schema levels, and enables one to utilize both conscious and unconscious processes. A nine-step therapeutic approach is presented as a suggested means of using this multischema model in therapy.*

In a prior paper this author compared cognitive therapy and Ericksonian hypnotherapy, finding a surprisingly wide range of similarities in approaches and techniques in these two important and seemingly so divergent psychotherapeutic frameworks (Feldman, 1988). Ericksonian hypnotherapy, a subset of the vast therapeutic techniques of Milton Erickson, generally involves the use of trance and indirect suggestion to bypass conscious awareness and utilize unconscious processes. In contrast, cognitive therapy focuses upon conscious processes, enabling the patient to identify and change dysfunctional patterns of thought. The concept of cognitive schema (Beck et al., 1979, p. 12) or internal maps

A significant portion of this paper was initially presented as an invited workshop at the Fourth International Congress on Ericksonian Hypnosis and Psychotherapy, December 1988. The author wishes to thank the Erickson Foundation for the impetus to formulate these ideas and the opportunity to present them at a professional forum of such high calibre.

Address correspondence to Jeffrey Feldman, Ph.D., Charlotte Rehabilitation, 1100 Blythe Blvd., Charlotte, NC 28203.

(Lankton & Lankton, 1983, p. 12) was presented as a conceptual bridge between these two schools of therapy. It was argued that Ericksonian hypnotherapy, working on an unconscious level, and cognitive therapy, working on a conscious level, follow different paths along the information processing continuum to generate change in dysfunctional schemas. While the author proposed that one can use both conscious and unconscious processes in effecting change in underlying schemas, and thereby more fully utilize the whole person, he did not indicate how one might actually do that.

The current paper builds upon the prior one, further developing the concept of cognitive schema into a multilevel construct. A model for using this multilevel construct in organizing a psychotherapeutic approach which integrates Ericksonian and cognitive therapies will then be presented.

Specifically, this paper will briefly review common features of Ericksonian hypnotherapy and cognitive therapy and discuss the fundamental difference between them. The concept of cognitive schema is reviewed and further developed into a model involving multilevel organization. How cognitive therapy and Ericksonian hypnotherapy operate according to the model is discussed. Common dysfunctional schemas at each level of the model are illustrated, as well as how the construction of metaphors, the use of indirect suggestion, and the formulation of therapeutic tasks follow from this model. Finally, a nine-step procedure for doing therapy that combines Ericksonian and cognitive techniques using this multilevel schema model is presented.

## Common Features of Ericksonian and Cognitive Therapy

This section briefly reviews the most salient commonalities between Ericksonian and cognitive therapies. These similarities were more fully discussed in this author's prior paper (Feldman, 1988), and are summarized in Table 1. Well-known principles and techniques associated with Ericksonian therapy are presented, and statements of cognitive therapists are cited to demonstrate points of agreement.

One of the primary principles of Ericksonian therapy is to individualize one's therapeutic approach. Similarly, cognitive therapists are instructed to "gear their approach to the level of the patient" (Beck, Rush, Shaw, & Emery, 1979, p. 169) and to tailor therapeutic interventions individually (Turk, Meichenbaum, & Genest, 1983, p. 347). The principle of utilization is also central to an Ericksonian approach. Beck and his colleagues wrote of the importance of "entering the patient's perspective and utilizing the patient's world view and idiosyncratic concepts" (Beck et al., 1979, p. 143).

---

Table 1
Common Elements of Ericksonian and Cognitive Approaches

---

*Therapeutic principles*
    Individualization of treatment
    Utilization of:
        Belief systems
        Patient's strengths
        Self
    Flexibility
    Persistence

*Therapeutic tactics and techniques*
    Behavioral intervention
    Metaphors
    Teaching tales
    Reframing
    Trance (relaxation, imagery)
    Future pacing (cognitive rehearsal, imagery rehearsal)
    Surprise
    Reduction of tasks to components

---

They also suggested that a patient's adaptive beliefs can be utilized in changing dysfunctional ones, and that "even the most difficult patient has strengths that can be used to offset antitherapeutic reactions" (Beck et al., 1979, p. 296). Furthermore, Erickson's wide-ranging use of himself in therapy is encouraged to an extent by cognitive therapists. "Selective self-disclosure" in the form of stories or anecdotes to activate affect in a patient was mentioned by Beck and his colleagues (Beck et al., 1979, p. 171), and Jeff Young, a noted cognitive therapist, evoking parallels to Erickson's "February man" case, wrote of using oneself in therapy as part of a "reparenting" process (Young, 1987, p. 62). Two other characteristics of an Ericksonian approach, flexibility (Lankton & Lankton, 1983, p. 21) and persistence, are also suggested as useful by cognitive therapists (Beck et al., 1979, pp. 296, 306).

Further congruence between these therapeutic approaches can be found in the realm of therapeutic techniques. Ericksonian strategic therapy often uses tasks designed to generate minimal strategic change. Similarly, cognitive therapists assign homework activities to generate environmental feedback contrary to dysfunctional beliefs, thereby disconfirming the patient's model of the world. Erickson is well known for his pioneering use of indirect suggestion and metaphor. Cognitive therapists have been instructed to use an "analogy which fits the patient" (Beck et al., 1979, p. 275), and if the patient is highly defended against learning new material, an indirect approach may be employed that provides information via stories and metaphors (Turk et al., 1983, pp. 187–188).

Reframing is a technique familiar to Ericksonian hypnotherapists and practitioners of Neurolinguistic Programming (NLP). It similarly is used in cognitive therapy when, for instance, a patient feels he or she has "failed" at a task and the experience is reframed as a source of data for devising other assignments. Indeed, as was argued previously by this author, cognitive therapy can be viewed as a structured format for reframing one's cognitions (Feldman, 1988, p. 612).

A trancelike state is most likely often induced by cognitive therapists when using relaxation and imagery techniques. Similarly, what hypnotherapists term "future pacing" or "future progression" is spoken of as "cognitive rehearsal" (Beck et al., 1979, p. 136) and "imagery rehearsal" (Turk et al., 1983, pp. 3–5) by cognitively oriented therapists. Furthermore, induced imagery, time projection, and symbolic imagery (metaphors) are familiar techniques to the Ericksonian practitioner of trance (see Beck & Emery, 1985, pp. 211–218). In addition, Emery specifically cites Erickson as a model for using surprise or "doing the unexpected" (Beck & Emery, 1985, p. 286).

Finally, in terms of therapeutic tactics, a clear parallel can be found to what the Lanktons (1983, p. 23) refer to as "reducing a task to component bits." In cognitive therapy, a large task is divided into small steps, and a relatively easy first step is given to the patient to start (Beck et al., 1979, p. 133).

The reader is referred to this author's prior paper for a more comprehensive discussion of stylistic differences and the relative degrees of agreement and disagreement between Ericksonian and cognitive therapy in the area of specific therapeutic principles (Feldman, 1988, pp. 62–64).

## The Fundamental Difference Between Ericksonian and Cognitive Therapy

To restate briefly the fundamental difference between cognitive therapy and Ericksonian hypnotherapy, cognitive therapy uses a highly rational, empirical approach, focusing on the conscious mind to generate change in conscious thought patterns and underlying systems of belief or schemas. In contrast, while Erickson worked with patients in and out of trance using both conscious and unconscious processes, Ericksonian hypnotherapy most often uses trance or indirect suggestion to bypass the limitations of the conscious mind and access unconscious resources. Trance is viewed as a context for change, and it is believed that therapeutic change can occur without conscious awareness as individuals utilize their own inner life experiences and associations to restructure themselves from within. In short, the basic difference between the two therapeutic approaches is the emphasis upon the conscious versus the unconscious mind.

## Cognitive Schemas—The Connecting Link

While cognitive therapy is viewed as operating on a conscious level and Ericksonian hypnotherapy on an unconscious level, they both work toward similar changes. Beck termed the focus of the change process "cognitive schemas," which guide an individual's perception, thinking, behavior, affect, and physiological responses (Beck et al., 1979, p. 12). Similarly, the Lanktons use the term "internal maps" by which an individual perceives the world and interprets or acts upon information. The Lanktons characterized a central therapeutic issue as follows: "Will therapy primarily work to edit or alter limiting aspects of the map which seem to either prevent desired behaviors or automatically produce unpleasant feeling states and unwanted behaviors? Or will therapy work to expand or elaborate the existing map to provide new experience or behavior?" (Lankton & Lankton, 1983, p. 12). In other words, both cognitive and Ericksonian therapy work to change these cognitive schemas or internal maps by which we select, interpret, and act upon information.

In a similar vein, Rossi wrote about consciousness or mind as "a process of self-reflective information transduction" (Rossi, 1986, p. 34). From this perspective, we may speak of schemas as the interpretive rules that guide information transduction. From the perspective of Ericksonian hypnotherapy, Rossi was alluding to the need to attend to these schemas consciously, and not to expect change to occur effectively on just an unconscious level, when he wrote, "The raw imagery of the right hemisphere is cooked or transduced by the left hemisphere" (Rossi, 1986, p. 83). In other words, the imagery and wealth of stored information accessed on an unconscious level via hypnotherapy will be filtered or interpreted through existing cognitive schemas.

Increasingly, the concept of schema is becoming recognized as a prominent theoretical element in psychodynamics, cognitive science, development psychology, and artificial intelligence (Horowitz, Stinsen, & Ruffini, 1989, p. 4). Figure 1 is presented to help clarify the central processing role of schemas and as a guide to further explanation below.

It should be noted that this is a highly simplified model of the complex multilevel selection and processing of information that take place at preconscious and conscious levels (Feldman, 1985, 1988). Nevertheless, it can serve to help elaborate the following general points about schemas: (1) schemas guide our perception by means of the selection and interpretation of information. (2) schemas, therefore, actively determine our behavior, thoughts, affect, and physiological responses. (3) schemas function recursively in that they receive feedback from our senses, behavior, thoughts, affect, and physiological responses. While this feedback generally confirms our schemas, it provides potential avenues for modifying schemas. For

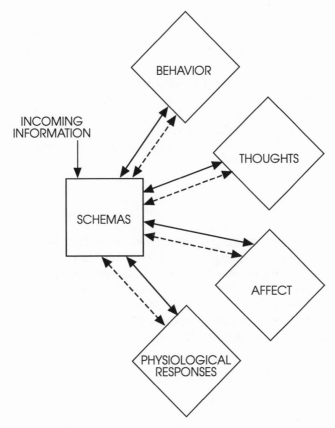

*Figure 1:* The central processing role of schemas.

instance, if I have the cognitive schema that I am a poor speaker, this will probably result behaviorally in my speaking stiffly and with frequent hesitations, and cognitively, in difficulties with thinking clearly and flexibly; my affect probably will be flat, and physiologically I will probably experience anxiety-related symptoms of a dry throat, shaking hands, and pounding heart. All of this will feed back to me, confirming this schema. If, on the other hand, I begin to perceive feedback from the audience in the form of smiles, head nods, or laughter when I expect it, and other signs of interest, then I will probably think that I am doing well, resulting in improved affect, decreased physiological response, and improved behavioral efficacy (i.e., quality of speaking). Therefore, as additionally illustrated in this example, we may note (4) that schemas are maintained in and help to maintain a social system.

Also, since the more typically relevant social system providing feedback is the family, (5) schemas are determined by developmental history. They develop in a family context as a means of making sense of the world and operating most safely and effectively in it. Moreover, since there are many dimensions to the world and oneself in it, (6) schemas tend to be complex, including multiple interacting levels. In general, it is easier consciously to access or be aware of schemas about the world and how to function in it than it is to access schemas about oneself. A probable exception is that some people who have been in analysis for a long time may have highly developed schemas about themselves, but not about the world and how to function in it. How schemas develop and function in relation to each other forms the basis for the model of multilevel schema organization to follow.

## The Structure of Cognitive Schemas

The model of multilevel cognitive schemas described here is a revision of the one presented by Guidano and Liotti (1983) in their landmark book, *Cognitive Processes and Emotional Disorders*. This author is deeply indebted to them and acknowledges their brilliant work. This author's revised model of cognitive schema organization is illustrated in Figure 2. Each level of schema organization in this model is described briefly and then more fully explained through clinical example.

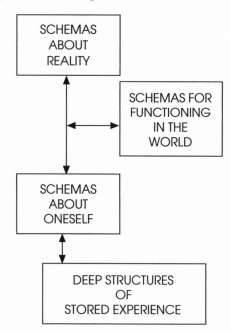

*Figure 2:* The structure of cognitive schemas. (Adapted from Guidano & Liotti, 1983)

The first level of schemas relates to those an individual has concerning external reality. This, of course, involves a tremendous range of organizing principles that enable one to make sense of the world. For brevity's sake, examples are limited to a few relevant to the generation of anxiety. These include schemas involving others and the nature of the world and its dangers. While Ellis has presented many of the classic dysfunctional or "irrational" beliefs, I will list for illustration some I have repeatedly seen in practice.

1. Others are out to get you—it's a hostile world.
2. There is an absolutely right and an absolutely wrong way to do something.
3. The world is a frustrating place.
4. Disaster can strike at any time.
5. Outsiders are dangerous.
6. Others will leave or reject you, especially if you express anger, make demands, or do not take care of all their needs.
7. Men will always leave you.
8. Women will trap you.
9. The harder something is to get, the better it is.

The second level of cognitive schemas to be discussed involves those about oneself. These primarily involve conceptualizations of one's self-identity and self-esteem (Guidano & Liotti, 1983, p. 68). Jeff Young and his colleagues at the New York Center for Cognitive Therapy have done seminal work in enumerating many of these dysfunctional self-schemas. They include (Young, 1987, pp. 10–15):

1. I am dependent and cannot function on my own.
2. I am defective and fundamentally unlovable by others.
3. I am incompetent; nothing I ever do is good enough.
4. I am fundamentally bad and don't deserve happiness.
5. I am entitled to anything I want and don't have to live by the rules of others.
6. I am fundamentally different from others.
7. I can involuntarily lose self-control.
8. I cannot be alone.
9. I cannot be too close to others or I will be suffocated.
10. I can never get my needs met.
11. I am highly vulnerable and cannot handle any stress.

While both schemas about oneself and about reality develop from and are linked to one's life experience, those about oneself are theorized as evolving from early and persistent communications and experience in one's family of origin. Schemas about oneself are most likely stored on an unconscious level. These early experiential data form deep structures of stored experience, or what Guidano and Liotti (1983, p. 63) call the "metaphysical hard core." This is analogous to what Rossi has referred to as "state-dependent encoded information" (Rossi, 1986, pp. 35–56), and what Erickson referred to as "early learning sets" ("all that you know, but don't know you know") (Erickson, Rossi, & Rossi, 1976, pp. 5–27). These deep structures of stored experience are generally based on early, often preverbal, experience, and are most likely encoded in episodic memory. What many refer to as this "right-brain" form of encoding tends to make these experiences and resulting deep structures accessible through imagery, fantasy, trance, and dreams.

In contrast, most of the schemas about reality and functioning in the world are learned later, often are verbally encoded, and are more accessible to "left-brain" accessing. In other words, they probably are preconsciously stored and available for the conscious mind to access. Therefore, while schemas generally function unconsciously, in the sense that one is not usually aware of them, it is much easier to become consciously aware of one's schemas about the world than of those about oneself.

The third set of schemas, those for functioning in the world, are probably easiest for the mental health professional to identify. This is true in part because these schemas readily follow from overt behavior and from the patient's thought processes while engaging in that behavior. One's schemas for functioning in the world develop from the interaction between schemas about reality and schemas about oneself. They also tend to be reinforced via environmental feedback, often in the form of a self-fulfilling prophecy. For instance, to return to the example of public speaking, relevant general schemas about reality might be that "others are out to get you or put you down." Relevant general schemas about oneself might involve a generally low level of self-esteem with an implicit feeling of vulnerability and a sense of being easily overwhelmed. More specific self-appraisals might identify oneself as being a poor speaker and as making a poor appearance. Given those interacting beliefs about others and oneself, one's general rule for operating in the world would be never to stick one's neck out, and specifically to avoid public speaking at all costs.

Common dysfunctional rules for operating in the world might develop through an interaction between schemas about reality and about oneself, as shown in Table 2.

The therapeutic usefulness of identifying the operative underlying schemas on these different levels is that it provides a conceptual blueprint for therapy. Based on an understanding of these implicit schemas, one can tailor therapeutic interventions to generate change, whether through therapeutic tasks, metaphors, or stories, or by direct cognitive evaluation and disconfirmation of the schemas. As will be discussed further, one can work on a number of levels of schema organization simultaneously using various techniques.

Table 2
The Interactive Development of Rules for Operating in the World

| Schemas About Reality × | Schemas About Oneself = | Rules for Operating in the World |
|---|---|---|
| 1. Others will leave you. | I'm unlovable. | Don't ever become emotionally involved. |
| 2. There's an absolutely right way to do things. | I'm not lovable for myself and only valued for what I do. | Always do things perfectly. |
| 3. Men will be men. | I can't be alone. | Accept whatever he does as long as he stays. |
| 4. The world is a hard, frustrating place. | I am vulnerable. | Do not become involved with others. |

For instance, one might work in a number of ways at changing a schema for operating in the world, which states, "Everything I do must be perfect." One can assign a task to do something not to perfection, such as cleaning the house incompletely before friends come over. The experience in the manner of cognitive therapy can then be evaluated in terms of thoughts evoked and the reality of consequences. One can tell a metaphor, in or out of trance, about Navajo rug weavers who always purposely weave one imperfection into their rugs because their religion tells them that only God is perfect. Or one can tell a story about two classmates in graduate school. One did a somewhat flawed dissertation, which suggested the need for further work in the field, and went on to a successful career, while the other is still looking for the perfect dissertation project. Similar techniques, such as having the patient do a task in two ways, can be used to change the schema about the world that there is an absolutely right way to do things. The ego-supportive stance of the therapist, the process of therapy, indirect or direct suggestions in or out of trance, insight-oriented work, and/or interpersonally oriented tasks once one is well along in therapy, synergistically work gradually to change an underlying schema that "I am unlovable for myself, and only valued for what I do."

## Clinical Examples of the Use of the Multischema Model

The following are two clinical cases presented to illustrate the use of this multilevel schema approach. The first will be briefly described, while the second will be presented at some length to illustrate a proposed therapeutic process that integrates Ericksonian and cognitive therapy approaches.

The first case involved a 23-year-old college graduate who was unemployed and moderately depressed. A settlement he had received for the death of his stepfather in a plane crash had put him in a financial position where he did not need to work. He nevertheless, somewhat reasonably, felt depressed and useless when not working. He felt unworthy of jobs he desired and felt that lesser jobs were unworthy of him. He was highly anxious at job interviews, especially when the interviewer was male, and he had not applied for a job in over a year. He felt ashamed of not working and avoided friends. Also, he would not do things he had enjoyed in the past because he felt that he did not deserve to do them if he was not working.

This patient's dysfunctional rules for operating in the world involved avoiding situations with other people in general, and, in particular, avoiding situations where he might be judged, evaluated, confronted, or threatened, especially by men. Dysfunctional schemas about the world included: (1) One is only as good as the job one does, with the specific corollary that people view you as a failure if you are not in a "fast-track" job. (2) All friends are in interesting fast-track jobs. (3) It's a dog-eat-dog world. (4) Men in particular are out to beat you, put you down, or be one up on you. (5) One does not deserve enjoyment without working.

The patient's negative view of men in general and of himself had developed from his life experience with an abusive, highly punitive stepfather. According to the patient, whatever he chose to do in a situation, his stepfather would always view as wrong, or find fault with and beat him. Relevant schemas that developed for this patient about himself from these early life experiences were: (1) I cannot trust my judgment. (2) I am a weak, ineffectual person. (3) I cannot stand criticism or rejection (i.e., it leads to terrible consequences). (4) I can easily be overwhelmed (i.e., destroyed), especially by men.

In capsule summary, treatment with this patient gradually involved elucidation of the above beliefs about himself and the world, and his rules for operating in it. Trance (relaxation) training was initiated to enable the patient to manage his anxiety sufficiently to be able to begin to carry out therapeutic tasks designed to test those beliefs. Interspersed among the relaxation training inductions were ego-supportive suggestions designed to begin indirectly to suggest change in underlying beliefs about himself and behavior (e.g., *"You can* become more *confident* in your *abilities* to manage how you feel and what you *do,* the more you practice this and develop your *extensive capabilities* to *relax* in this way"). In addition, the consistent stance of the older male therapist conveying the presumption that the patient was a bright, competent, creative young man naturally contributed, through the psychotherapeutic process, to the changing of self concepts.

Tasks designed to challenge his beliefs about the world and rules for operating in it were introduced in a graded fashion. Through social contacts with friends from college (initially women), he came to learn that others did not view him as a failure. Further, most of the jobs his friends had were far less glamorous, interesting, or fast track than he thought, and a few friends were interested in working with him in some way. Working in his sister's business in an increasingly responsible role helped to build self-confidence and a sense of competence. Also, reinvolvement in previous sources of enjoyment and accomplishment (skiing, soccer) helped to change his beliefs about the total importance of work and about himself.

While progress was being made on a number of fronts, a great deal of anxiety and avoidance behaviors continued to be exhibited in relation to men, especially those who were older or in positions of authority. The patient would, for instance, avoid interviews with males, often hanging up the phone if a man answered when he was calling to inquire about a job. A significant breakthrough did not come until, in trance, the patient relived some of the traumatic events of his childhood with his stepfather, but as an adult. The patient chose to stand up physically to his stepfather and overpower him, and from an adult perspective, was able to see his stepfather as an insecure, rigidly limited, and pathetic figure, rather than as the all-powerful, overwhelming figure of his childhood. Through reliving and reframing these stored experiential data in this way, dramatic changes occurred in the patient's self concept (schemas about self) and in his schemas about other men. This enabled him to test his internalized rules about dealing with men, to find out that many were not as hostile as he thought, and eventually to change his behavior. Through a series of increasingly positive experiences, he was able to change his concepts of himself further, and to open his own business. In this author's view, this change would not have taken place using a purely cognitive-behavioral approach. The hypnotic approach, involving a change or reframing of stored experiences, was needed to enable necessary changes in schemas about the self and others (men) to occur. Conversely, these schemas also probably would not have changed without the testing of reality inherent in a cognitive-behavioral carrying out of therapeutic tasks and subsequent cognitive appraisal of reality.

## A Proposed Therapeutic Model Integrating Ericksonian and Cognitive Approaches

Erickson taught that there should be as many different therapeutic approaches as there are patients (Lankton & Lankton, 1983, p. ii).

Nevertheless, this author has found some general steps that are helpful to keep in mind when attempting to combine elements of Ericksonian and cognitive approaches in psychotherapy. These steps, as delineated in Table 3, represent an expansion of the process of cognitive therapy (Beck et al., 1979; Guidano & Liotti, 1983, pp. 304–305). This author suggests that this be viewed as a general outline, open to flexible and creative changes, rather than as a rigid blueprint for therapy. A clinical example illustrates the use of these steps in psychotherapy.

---

Table 3
A Proposed Therapeutic Model Integrating Ericksonian
and Cognitive Approaches

---

1. Evaluation
2. Task(s) to identify dysfunctional cognitions
3. Appraisal of the most relevant cognitions (beliefs)
4. Introduction of trance
5. Ongong triggering, evaluation, and challenging of schemas
6. Inquiry concerning determinants of schemas
7. Appraisal of relevant underlying schemas about the self
8. Ongoing use of therapeutic techniques of multilevel schema change
9. Evaluation of progress and of future alternatives

---

In addition to the cognitive therapists cited above, I also am indebted to the patient I will briefly present as an illustration of the use of this model in psychotherapy. Her ongoing drive to heal herself through painfully honest self-appraisal, effort, humor, and loving testing of herself and others taught me more than is possible to learn from books. The thumbnail sketch presented cannot do justice to her or to the complexity of the therapeutic process.

As any therapeutic approach would suggest, the first step in treatment involves evaluation. An effort at multimodal or multisystem assessment is suggested, with the domains of behavior, cognition, affect, physiological reactivity, and the social system being evaluated. The best structured assessment tool for this, to this author's knowledge, is Arnold Lazarus' Multimodal Life History Questionnaire. (Multimodal Publications, Inc., P.O. Box 551, Kingston, NJ 08528). Further evaluation includes a determining of the individual's strengths, resources, and what Erickson called patterns of happiness. A therapist can begin to hypothesize dysfunctional schemas in this initial assessment phase that will become more fully apparent as therapy proceeds. Finally, the therapist needs to define the presenting problem to the patient in terms he or she can understand and accept, and they must mutually agree on a therapeutic goal.

The case in point was that of a 32-year-old married woman who worked as a nurse administrator in a neighborhood hospital in New York City. She presented with physiological symptoms of migraine headache, chronic muscle tension, fatigue, mild obesity, and the grinding of her teeth at night. She described herself as feeling angry a good deal of the time, and as generally feeling overwhelmed. Cognitively, she indicated that she was primarily angry at a supervisor at work, whom she also considered a friend, and at her husband. Behaviorally, she tended to overcommit herself at work and with her family, taking on a caretaker role with others. She would overeat in response to stress, fatigue, and her feelings of being overwhelmed. In a manner not uncommon in Italian-American neighborhoods in New York, she lived in the upper story of a two-family house, above her in-laws. The patient was a highly conscientious, dependable woman of considerable strengths, including intelligence, good organizational skills, an empathic nature, and a good sense of humor. She indicated that, in addition to relief from her physiological symptoms, she would like to be able to deal with and express her anger better. She also said that throughout her life she felt that she had always been doing "everything she should." She had difficulty with identifying patterns of happiness, and said that she wanted to explore herself and what she really wanted. To hypothesize underlying schemas involving a large number of "shoulds" did not require great insight. It was agreed that we would work toward the relief of physiological symptoms and their underlying causes, including the patterns of thinking generating them. We also would work to help her to understand herself better and to develop the ability to make choices in her life according to what she wanted for herself.

To assess and identify dysfunctional cognitive schemas further, the patient was assigned a number of tasks (step 2). In a manner common to cognitive therapy, she was asked to describe and record her automatic thoughts whenever she felt tension and/or anger. She was also asked to make a list of every statement she could think of that might begin, "I should. . . ." Also, as a means of testing her capability for change and to seed notions of flexibility and future change of problematic behavior and thoughts, she was asked to do her laundry on a different day than the one on which she felt she always "should" do it.

From her extensive list of "shoulds" and recorded automatic thoughts, the following general underlying rules for operating in the world were abstracted: (1) I should always do for others. (2) Everything I do should be perfect. (3) I should always be doing something useful. (4) I should never express anger. This uncovering or appraisal with the patient of the most relevant underlying cognitions (step 3) provided a clearer focus for therapy.

Simultaneous with the above evaluative process was the introduction of trance (step 4) in the latter part of each therapeutic session. This was introduced in the context of beginning to cope with stressors and to change the physiological response patterns that generated chronic muscle tension, fatigue, grinding of teeth, and migraine headaches. The patient's increasing ability to utilize trance or relaxation techniques enabled her to cope with the anxiety generated by progressively assigned tasks to challenge "shoulds." In an effort to develop further therapeutic leverage, indirect suggestions were interspersed during trance to suggest ego strengthening, change, taking time for and caring for herself, enjoyment, and freedom. Also, trying different techniques (because there was no right or wrong way to relax) and allowing time for herself to relax from effortful activity were particularly useful in the change of schemas involving always doing for others, always doing things perfectly and always being useful. (See the appendix, p. 72, for the text of an induction.)

Ongoing triggering, evaluation, and challenging of schemas (step 5) characterize the process that develops next in therapy. While this might involve the assignment of specific therapeutic tasks, in the case of this patient, real-life events that triggered anger and anxiety were brought into therapy sessions. For instance, on one occasion, the patient's father called, asking her to take care of some financial and legal matters for him. Previously, she would have operated under the schema, "I always take care of others as the responsible, competent one in the family." In a manner characteristic of cognitive therapy, she was taught to assess the validity of that inner statement. She was able to ascertain that, in reality, her father could take care of the matters when he came up from Florida, or her brother, an attorney, could certainly handle them. Further, in the cognitive therapy tradition of finding alternative ways of looking at it, she was able to change this schema to: "I am indeed a responsible, competent person and can handle what I choose to handle. If I take care of everyone else all the time, I can't take care of myself." Similarly, the patient was able to deal with the anxiety about getting to work exactly on time generated by her perfectionistic inner rules. She was able to acknowledge that the reality of the situation was that nothing depended on her being there exactly at 8:30, that she was indeed on time virtually every day, and with the variances of New York City traffic, everyone would understand her being a few minutes late on occasion. She was also able to look at the alternative perspective that she now was an administrative professional who often worked late, and that in such a position, one does not punch a clock.

In the course of therapy, this author finds it relatively natural eventually to steer inquiry toward the developmental determinants of the identified dysfunctional schemas (step 6). This can be done by such simple inquiry as asking the patient, "Why might you have come to believe that?"

In the case of this patient, the development of the rules about the reality of her experiential world was relatively easy to uncover, because these rules had been most intensely apparent during her latency and teenage years. When she was of latency age, her mother had a heart attack, and she and the family lived with the awareness and effects of her heart condition until the patient's early adult years. The patient took the role of a helper substitute for her mother in the family, with the accompanying responsibilities and rules. For the patient, these rules held the emotional force of possibly causing her mother's death if they were broken. For instance, the schema about perfection developed from the implicit and explicit communications to her to the effect that "if you don't do it right (i.e., the way your mother would), your mother will have to redo it" (and that could kill her). The rule about always doing for others logically followed from the expectation that "you need to take care of things for your mother." The notion that she should always be doing something useful evolved from the communication that "there is always something productive you can do" (i.e., so your mother won't have to). Finally, the prohibition against expressing anger was the consequence of the great emotional upset that such expression would cause her mother. The patient reported an instance when, in anger, she had slammed a door at home, and her father removed all the doors in the house, and kept them off for a time.

The above ongoing experiences provide, according to this multilevel schema model, the experiential data from which an individual's rules about reality in his or her social system, as well as schemas about himself or herself, evolve. To elucidate these underlying schemas about the self (step 7), when such experiences are discussed, this author tends to use such straightforward techniques as asking, "So how did that make you feel about yourself?" In this case, the patient apparently developed a view of herself as a responsible, caring, and competent person. This was generated, though, by a negative sense of self in which (on a deeper level) she believed that she was not valued for herself, but valued for what she did and how well she did it for others. In related fashion, the patient viewed herself as unattractive and unappealing. This in part appeared to be generated by the inherent threat of her adolescence, and the increased probability of her being taken from the family if she appealed to young men. In a number of ways, her family, therefore, without conscious intent, encouraged her overeating and discouraged adolescent dating activity. In the context of her life situation during the time of therapy, as the patient began to lose weight and to dress and view herself differently, this predictably generated anxiety in her husband.

As any reader with a minimal amount of experience doing psychotherapy knows, the therapeutic process does not take a linear form, as the presented model might seem to imply. This is perhaps most apparent in considering the next step listed (step 8), the ongoing use of therapeutic techniques for multilevel schema change. This corresponds to what traditionally is referred to in psychotherapy as working through. The utility of this multilevel schema model at this stage is that it provides a conceptual framework for simultaneously working on a number of levels, using both conscious and unconscious processes. On a conscious level, the patient was well able to apply the empirical approach of cognitive therapy, examining the reality of the situation and the evidence for her anxiety-related thoughts. The patient was similarly able to rehearse alternative ways of thinking about herself and situations. A verbal flash card method was developed in which in response to feelings of anxiety or anger, the patient would flash the letters o, p, and u to remind her to assess whether those feelings were related to her underlying schemas of always doing for others, of being perfect, or of always doing something useful. Certain behavioral tasks were also assigned, such as going to the zoo to spend a day without useful intent. On another day, she took an unplanned, and so not perfectly prepared for, trip to the beach. The patient was also encouraged to inquire about flying lessons: this interest had developed partly because of her father's military career, but she could not pursue it owing to her sex and her role in the family. Flying became a metaphor alluded to with a number of associated issues during the course of treatment.

In addition to the use of flying, other metaphors were tailored to different levels of schema organization. For instance, in terms of herself and her self concept, the metaphor of a flowering plant, long dormant, but whose bud was now beginning to open, was presented. Stories about great discoveries ensuing from experimental errors and the Navajo weaver story, previously described, were presented to suggest the unrealistic and undesirable aspect of her schemas about perfection.

Other Ericksonian techniques, in addition to indirect suggestion mentioned above, were used both in and out of trance. To help change her schema about always doing for others, not always taking care of others was reframed as a caring approach because it enabled others to better care for themselves. Future pacing (cognitive rehearsal) was used outside of trance to rehearse certain conversations and scenarios with others, as well as in trance to enable the patient to experience flying and other wishes. Some therapeutic reparenting was done in trance to modify the patient's deep structures of stored experience. This involved reliving certain key events, with her parents acting in a more appropriate manner towards her in relation to her age and developmental level.

Furthermore, the therapeutic process, in which the therapist took a supportive stance, consistently communicating to the patient that she, herself, was an individual of value and had a right to a more fulfilling and enjoyable life in the ways she chose, was in and of itself highly therapeutic. These new life experiences associated with therapy implicitly contradicted previously developed schemas about the patient and her relationships to others in the world, allowing for the development of revised deep structures. These experiences helped the patient to change her patterns of interacting with members of her social system, which tended to reinforce her previous schemas. This, of course, was a difficult process, strongly resisted by others, as the patient made changes in her relationships with her husband, father, brother, in-laws, and friends.

In common with all therapeutic approaches, the termination phase of therapy involves a review of progress to date and a look at future alternatives (step 9). The multilevel schema model can be helpful for patients in terms of reviewing the changes made in their thinking about themselves, the world, and their previously held rules for operating in it, and the behaviors that followed from those rules. For this patient, the gradual elimination of physiological symptoms accompanied her changes in thought and behavior. A significant change in her weight and appearance also accompanied her changes in her self concept. Her ongoing battle with making changes in her relationship with family members was facilitated by a planned move with her husband to a small midwestern city, where he would do graduate study. Future alternatives were discussed with the patient, with the conclusion that, in the short term, doing less with regard to her career would enable her to do more for herself. Parting suggestions, confidently affirming the patient's continuing ability to utilize what had been learned and to make changes on her own, constituted the last intervention, which was probably one of the more important therapeutic interventions made.

## Concluding Remarks

While a good patient can make a therapeutic approach seem better than it is, the above case was presented to illustrate the utility of this multischema model and to suggest a procedure for its implementation. The notion of cognitive schemas has been presented as a conceptual bridge between two of the most powerful psychotherapeutic approaches available—cognitive therapy and Ericksonian hypnotherapy. This recognition of compatibility makes the vast array of therapeutic techniques from both schools of therapy available to the clinician. It further brings greater conceptual clarity to Ericksonian work, while increasing the applicability of a cognitive approach to a broader range of patients. These might include persons with personality disorders or other psychological disturbances related to their developmental histories for whom cognitive therapy approaches are beginning to be modified and applied.

The multilevel schema model presented provides a conceptual basis for understanding the great difficulty generally encountered in attempting to change a patient's dysfunctional patterns of thought and behavior. Even the simplest surface belief is a product of a multidetermined interaction between an individual's beliefs about the world and about himself or herself. These beliefs are rooted in, or evolve from, early and often persistent life experiences, which generally are stored on an unconscious level. In addition, these beliefs tend to be reinforced or reconfirmed by the feedback of ongoing experience in the form of self-fulfilling prophecies.

The multilevel schema model further provides a framework for evaluation and intervention that takes into account these complex interactions and utilizes both conscious and unconscious processes. In so doing, it assesses not only current behavior and accompanying patterns of cognition, but also the personal history and past and present family systems instrumental in the development and maintenance of dysfunctional schemas. In this way, this multischema model has the potential for further generating bridges to psychodynamic and family-systems–oriented therapies. Suggestions were made in this regard in the nine-step procedures presented. This author awaits the further development and application of multischema models and procedures by some of the dedicated and creative people working to expand the domains of cognitive and Ericksonian therapies.

## Appendix
## Trance Induction

Take the time you really need for yourself now to make the changes you need to make within yourself, to shift from your usually highly aware, alert, other-oriented way of being to a more comfortable, relaxed, inner-focused way of being that comes when you allow everything else to fade away. As you focus upon yourself and the increasingly pleasant feelings that develop as effortlessly, you become more and more relaxed and comfortable with yourself. Allowing yourself to really enjoy how comfortable you can feel—how comfortable you can be with yourself when you let go of all excess tension, all excess burdens, and allow yourself the pleasure of breathing deeply and easily; allowing your muscles to relax—and as they relax, you may feel a warm, pleasant feeling or a tingling feeling inside yourself, in your hands or your feet—because, as the muscles relax, they allow for an increased ease of circulation—a desirable freedom of flow that you may feel within yourself—and I wonder just how it may feel to you to feel free of excess pressure in this way—I wonder how you can let yourself be—and why not allow yourself to be as comfortable as you can, knowing that it's an interesting as well as pleasurable type of learning—that you can hold onto all that's important within yourself while letting go of all that's important for you to let go of—letting go of all excess tension, all discomfort, all excess pressures and burdens. Knowing that each and every time you practice this, you can become more and more comfortable in this way, more and more comfortable with yourself and more and more confident in your abilities to relax and let go and become comfortable. As you become more and more confident in yourself and your abilities to become comfortable in this way, it feels more and more natural and easy just being comfortable with yourself in this way, and the interesting thing is that just as the experience is different for each person, and every time you practice this, the experience is somewhat different—sometimes becoming more relaxed, sometimes becoming more aware of how you feel, sometimes enjoying yourself in pleasant memories, sometimes becoming aware from within yourself what's really most important for you to look at now. It really doesn't matter how deeply you go, so there is no exactly right way to do this—no wrong way—nothing to measure up to—which in knowing that there is no exactly right way to be—can free you—to be and explore yourself in a new way—finding what's right for you by simply allowing yourself to be comfortable—being yourself—in this way—and being curious about how good you can feel. Nothing you need to try to do, nothing you need to think about, nothing you need to feel; what most people have to learn is how to try not to try—and it's a curious paradox—how you can do what's most beneficial and useful for yourself in a way by not trying to do anything at all—just taking some time for yourself in this way—learning what's most important and helpful for you, by allowing yourself to let go of trying, and enjoying an incredible lightness of being that allows you to breathe freely, deeply, easily, and effortlessly.

## References

Beck, A. J., & Emery, G. (1985). *Anxiety disorders and phobias: A cognitive perspective.* New York: Basic Books.

Beck, A. J., Rush, A. J., Shaw, B. F., Jr., & Emery, G. (1979). *Cognitive therapy of depression.* New York: Guilford Press.

Erickson, M. H., Rossi, E., & Rossi, S. (1976). *Hypnotic Realities* (pp. 5–27). New York: Irvington.

Feldman, J. (1985). Subliminal perception and information processing theory: Empirical and conceptual validation of Erickson's notion of the unconscious. In J. Zeig (Ed.), *Ericksonian psychotherapy, Volume I: Structures* (pp. 431–447). New York: Brunner/Mazel.

Feldman, J. (1988). A comparison of Ericksonian and cognitive therapies. In S. Lankton & J. Zeig (Eds.), *Ericksonian Monographs, Number 4, Research, comparisons and medical applications of Ericksonian techniques* (pp. 57–73). New York: Brunner/Mazel.

Guidano, V. F., & Liotti, G. (1983). *Cognitive processes and emotional disorders: A structural approach to psychotherapy.* New York: Guilford Press.

Horowitz, M. J., Stinsen, C. O., & Ruffini, J. (1989). Program summary: Program on conscious and unconscious processes. San Francisco: Center for the Study for the Neuroses, Langley Porter Psychiatric Institute, University of California at San Francisco.

Lankton, S., & Lankton, C. (1983). *The answer within: A clinical framework of Ericksonian hypnotherapy.* New York: Brunner/Mazel.

Rossi, E. (1986). *The psychology of mind–body healing: New concepts of therapeutic hypnosis.* New York: Norton.

Turk, D. C., Meichenbaum, D., & Genest, M. (1983). *Pain and behavioral medicine: A cognitive-behavioral perspective.* New York: Guilford Press.

Young, J. (1987). Schema-focused cognitive therapy for personality disorders. New York: Cognitive Therapy Center of New York (unpublished manuscript).

# "Ironic" Therapy:
# Utilizing Unconscious Conflict
# in Single-Session Hypnotherapy

## Janet Sasson Edgette, Psy.D.

*This article discusses the separate hypnotherapies of two adults, each of which were successfully conducted in a single session. One involves a psychotherapist in her 30s seeking the psychological liberty to move into independent practice, and the other involves a 45-year-old loan officer who developed an eating disorder in response to changes in his work environment. In each case discussion, I identify what I consider likely to have been the pivotal intervention. Deep trance states were used, and the therapy was directed at unconscious levels of psychological functioning. These two cases illustrate a probable way to make dynamic and even characterological shifts simply by using hypnosis to change the nature of the relationship between an intrapsychic conflict and the presenting symptom. Although the mutative intervention is not consciously identified by the client, its impact is both significant and enduring.*

Successful single-session case studies are always interesting, but they become even more so when we think we know what effected the positive change. The following cases describe the treatment of two adults who presented with very different problems, both focal, however, in nature. In each case, an intervention was designed to change the pathogenic relationship between the symptom or problem and that facet of the client's personality that maintained it. Thus, in lieu of trying to modify character structure or intervene with the symptom itself, therapy takes place via an efficient shift in how these two phenomena are psychologically connected. The connection altered, the symptom can then be let go as it no longer has the same meaning or purpose. The client moves ahead.

In each of the cases discussed, the client is held back from meeting his or her goals by a pronounced, yet unconscious, intrapsychic conflict. This

Address correspondence to Janet Sasson Edgette, Psy.D., Milton H. Erickson Institute, 1062 Lancaster Ave., Rosemont Plaza, Rosemont, PA 19010.

kind of factor intrigues me tremendously as a clinician, and my initial diagnostic assessments reflect my belief that such issues, undetected and unaddressed, can often stymie a therapist who has an otherwise accurate pulse reading on the case, as well as thoughtfully developed interventions. But in the context of single session or brief therapy, intrapsychic conflict adds an especially interesting dimension; because of the concentrated energies with which it holds a "symptom" in place and repels more adaptive behaviors and attitudes, significant changes can be abruptly and nearly completely effected by altering the *valences*, so to speak, of these healthy and unhealthy behaviors. An incisive psychological intervention can effect this alteration, allowing the conflict, still unconscious, to attract a different and "better" symptom. Somnambulistic trance work provides a perfect arena for such untethering and retethering of behavior/affect/ defense.

## Survivor's Guilt

Elena was an accomplished, personable, and bright psychologist in her mid-30s who sought therapy to help her overcome bouts of anxiety generated by considerations of professional advancement. She specifically wanted to make the move into private practice from her position as staff therapist at a residential treatment center for emotionally disturbed adolescents. She had been in the field for some time, had developed a good reputation, and had established a wide network of colleagues and other referral sources to support a practice. But despite this groundwork and a strong (conscious) feeling of a readiness to move on, Elena was unable to take concrete steps toward setting up an independent practice. Thoughts of giving notice at the treatment center, designing business cards, or renting office space filled her with anxiety, as did the idea of informing colleagues of her plans. She was having difficulty sleeping at night and rapidly losing what had been a long-standing sense of self-assurance and competence.

During the initial diagnostic session, Elena told her story of having grown up in a South American country during a time of civil strife and war. Her family had had their home and property taken away from them several times over, and had endured years of ethnic torment and political occupation. Issues of safety and security were paramount. However, Elena, being an exceptionally resourceful individual, fared considerably better than her other family members, both in their country of origin and in their subsequent adjustment following their move to the United States several years later. As Elena's resiliency and adaptability increasingly became assets in her new home, and as she began to orchestrate a better, more personally and professionally gratifying life for herself than her parents and siblings were experiencing, she became more and more emotionally conflicted. Feeling undeserving of solo achievements and as though she were leaving everyone else behind, Elena, unwittingly, had begun to truncate her own growth.

It was this particular dynamic, unconscious and tenacious, that was going to be the largest stumbling block for Elena in attaining her goals. While other issues, such as those concerning safety, stability, familiarity, and control, were important, none had the power to brake forward movement as did this conflict over her having recovered from the traumas of war and moved on. "Things are too good (for me)," Elena would say, and then follow it up with spontaneous denials of any need to punish herself. That her dilemma was still largely unconscious was apparent in her musings, "What am I getting out of this (not moving ahead)? It doesn't make sense that I'm doing this to myself."

The dynamic was clear, and seemingly so was an appropriate intervention. The hypnotherapy thus was organized around making the idea of a successful independent practice *appealing*, rather than noxious, to that relevant aspect of her unconscious, her superego. If Elena could be convinced, at that level of psychological functioning, that the experience of independent practice was in fact consistent with her need to keep elements of hardship in her life, she would likely be able to embrace the idea more fully. And so, while she was in a very deep trance during the one hypnosis treatment session, Elena was told about all the ways in which private practice is *punishingly grueling*. Supportive interventions to this primary one included direct but obtuse suggestions to Elena that *her unconscious could relax now because it will still get what it thinks it needs*, and that *she could really rise to this new occasion (of private practice), although, of course, it would be very hard work.* Other interventions not directly related to this central one included those designed to remind Elena of her resourcefulness and her ability *to triumph in situations of adversity.*

I ran into Elena one year after this work was done. She waved at me from across a conference room and gave me a thumbs up sign. A brief conversation revealed that her private practice was booming, and her enjoyment of it was immense.

## Big Man Around Town

Ryan was a loan officer in his mid-40s who called for hypnotherapy for his "eating disorder." He had begun overeating six months previously, was binge eating, and had gained 20 pounds.

A brief history revealed that exactly six months prior to his contact with me, the bank in which he worked had issued an edict prohibiting smoking in the building. Ryan had imagined that he would at least have been able to continue smoking in the privacy of his own office, but this was not the case. Angered at having had "something taken away" from him by his boss, as he perceived it, Ryan began to hang out in the basement of the building, wasting company time. Ryan was aware of this little bit of acting out. His more strident act of passive-aggressive rebellion, however, was only partially understood by him, and would become manifest at the company-sponsored lunches served regularly during staff meetings. It was here that Ryan would assert his rights, eating his fill of company food. And while he was aware of how gratifying it was for him to eat all the boss's food, he wasn't aware of how gratifying it was, despite the discomfort, to eat so much that he had to find a private room in which to let out his belt a hole or two, and thus finally feel himself to be the "biggest man around."

That this man was experiencing considerable conflict with regard to issues of autonomy, control, and authority was obvious. But he was functioning adequately in his life, and did not seek out or ask me for a therapy through which he could learn such things about himself. He simply wanted to get over what he saw, pure and simple, as his eating disorder, and he wanted to do this as quickly as possible. I thought it likely that if eating large amounts of food in front of one's boss could become reconstrued as acquiescent, and the rejection of his food as an assertion of autonomy, the unconscious logjam supporting the symptom of overeating could be dispersed.

The primary intervention, therefore, was a story, told during a period of somnambulistic trance, about a male model (a character chosen specifically to appeal to Ryan's apparent, though inoffensive, vanity) who is making a commercial for a breakfast cereal (an item chosen for its rather regressive innuendo). The male director on the job is obnoxiously authoritarian and overbearing; he makes the model do dozens of retakes, every one of which requires the ingestion of another spoonful of cereal. I speak to my patient about *how that model tells himself, "You're not going to let that boss influence you to make yourself feel disgusted, are you?"* The story ends with the model's sudden thrust toward self-respect and autonomy, when he refuses to eat any more of his boss's food. *"And didn't he now feel like the big man about town!"* Another intervention supporting this included the setup of the trance work; since being a "big" man was important to Ryan, I started the induction with caveats that the therapeutic work involved for him would be a "mighty tall order," an intervention Zeig discusses in his material on diagnostic interviewing and treatment planning (1988).

Not imagining that this would be all the therapy required, we set up an appointment for a second hypnosis session. A few days before the scheduled appointment, Ryan called to cancel it, remarking, "I don't understand exactly what happened, but I think we took care of the problem. I don't think I need to come in!"

# Summary

The presenting problem in each of these cases could have been therapeutically challenged in any number of ways. In the case of Elena, another therapist might have done more with resource retrieval, helping her to renew feelings of resiliency, flexibility, and control over her destiny. Or future progression might have been an avenue pursued. With Ryan, pattern interruption, self-hypnosis, strategic task assignments, or rituals all could have been viable choices. But my interest in the role of psychodynamics in a client's psychological functioning often leads me to assess problems in terms of impulse, conflict, and defense, and I see these, too, as part of the playing field when considering what kind of hypnotherapy to do. The therapies described did nothing to ameliorate the unconscious conflict itself, nor did they illuminate issues much, if at all, for the clients. They just got them over their problems.

The problem of symptom substitution has often been an argument raised in discussions of these types of cases where there is abatement of the symptom or symptom complex without benefit of psychological insight. In most cases this seems specious. Many symptoms can be construed as behaviors, thoughts, or affects at one end of a continuum between adaptation and maladaptation. Since the dynamics, in Elena's case, surrounding survivor guilt remain unconsciously operative, there is always the possibility that she will stunt her growth or self-sabotage in other areas of her life unrelated to the practice of psychotherapy. But this seems less a comment on the superficialty of treatment than on the utter pervasiveness, in personality, of neurosis. The same could be said for Ryan, inasmuch as correcting the habit of overeating will probably not prevent him from acting out his struggles with autonomy and control in settings other than the bank's cafeteria. The point here is that he no longer feels out of control with regard to his eating and weight.

Another thought, though, is that we, as clinicians, have learned that the effects of therapy on a primary symptom can often have secondary, ripple effects throughout the individual's psyche and/or family and social system. Erickson was frequently known to have skill intervening in ways that resounded positively at many levels of clients' emotional and interpersonal functioning. This is a far more inviting, not to mention efficient, notion of recovering mental health than those likening psychopathology to a cancer whose every cell must be excised from the body for the person to be declared once again healthy.

It has been my unfortunate impression that practitioners of non-psychodynamic brief therapy have lost sight of the potential usefulness of psychodynamics in all types of therapy. Capitalizing on such concepts to expedite therapeutic change can happen outside of the conduction of psychodynamically oriented treatment in a relatively seamless fashion. There are times when clinicians' treatment of the concepts border on scorn, and throwing away theory like that is akin to throwing the "baby out with the bath water." This seems like a shame.

Only Elena can rightfully determine if she is better off with the new constellation of behaviors reflecting a conceptualization of independent practice as grueling. There is too, of course, the consideration that her psyche may organize itself around the intervention in more or less functional ways. Elena could embrace the hardships involved in building and maintaining a practice by responding with industry and zeal. Or she could, less adaptively, practice in a fashion that invites abuse on the part of patients. My understanding of her character and interpersonal style suggested that the deck was stacked in favor of the former.

I find it acceptable to work on problems as presented by the client on levels unknown by the client. I also believe that it is not incumbent upon me to provide more therapy than a client asks for. I may offer it, if indicated or if the situation is urgent, and I may impose it, if the situation is dangerous. The client, then, barring extraordinary clinical conditions, becomes more responsible for declaring how much therapy is enough. Too many therapists spend too much effort trying to "sell the customer up" to the next, higher (i.e., more thorough) model of therapy.

The Zeitgeist of psychotherapy has changed in the last decade and it has impelled many therapists to press out against established skill levels with sometimes novel results. Naturally, new questions related to how we practice our craft arise. For instance, there are ethical considerations in conducting a therapy in which the nature and agent of change remain outside of a client's awareness. These are metapsychological and multifaceted, and are covered in detail elsewhere (Edgette, 1988). For now, it is enough to say that newer, brief forms of treatment that alleviate clients' subjective emotional distress challenge many long-held beliefs about what are and are not essential parts and phenomena of a successful therapeutic process.

## References

Edgette, J. S. (1988). Tempest in a teapot: Ethics and Ericksonian approaches. In Lankton, S. (Ed.), *Ericksonian monographs, No. 5: Ericksonian hypnosis: Application, preparation and research*. New York: Brunner/Mazel.
Zeig, J. K. (1988). Workshop: Ericksonian psychotherapy and hypnosis. Philadelphia.

# Introduction to the Case: A Woman with Chronic Anxiety and Panic Attacks

## Stephen R. Lankton, M.S.W., D.A.H.B.

This was the first and only session of brief therapy for a 37-year-old woman with anxiety attacks and deep despair. She had presented herself to the agency a year and a half earlier (October 1989), but attended only a few sessions before ending therapy at that time. This session took place in May 1991. She arrived because of concerns about anxiety attacks, hopelessness, and despair, which were, for her, chronic and at times acute.

Joan's history, as given to me by her previous therapist, is as follows. She is divorced, is the mother of one son, and lives alone. Her mother died when Joan was three years of age. She has two older brothers. After her mother's death, she was raised by her grandmother, and her father paid little attention to her. Upon his remarriage, his new wife soon became pregnant, and her time was spent on concerns other than my client. Consequently, as a girl, Joan was close to her grandmother as a sort of mother substitute.

Unfortunately, her grandmother died when my client was 11 years old. When she was in her late teens, she eloped in order to leave home, but the relationship was an abusive one, and it lasted less than one year. She held various jobs, including those of a flight attendant and of a waitress. During this period, she had one aborted pregnancy from a seven-year relationship. In her 20s, she remarried. She had a son at the age of 25 and was divorced at the age of 30. Soon after, she lost custody of her son to her ex-husband as a result of her (self-proclaimed) drug abuse and sexual promiscuity.

Joan has been drug-free for years now, and is dating only one man. This man lives several hundreds of miles away in an apartment above that of

Address correspondence to Stephen R. Lankton, M.S.W., D.A.H.B., P.O. Box 958, Gulf Breeze, FL 32562.

his mother (this is also the man with whom Joan earlier had had a terminated pregnancy); consequently, she is often alone. This solitude is broken each summer when her son, now 10 years old, visits for a few weeks. The time is approaching (four weeks away) for his next visit, and this brings her additional anxiety and dread.

She recently was diagnosed with hepatitis B and had been hospitalized for four weeks. While in the hospital, she was visited by her father, and he informed her, for the first time, that her mother had died of hepatitis B (and not of a heart attack, as she had thought). Fortunately, she had not concluded that she too might die and thus fulfill her dreaded fear that some sort of doom would befall her. Quite the contrary, she was pleased to have had a meaningful talk with her father, which answered long-held questions about the mother's death.

This, again, was the background brought to me by this client, who presented her problem as almost unbearable feelings of anxiety, dread, hopelessness, and worthlessness.

## Follow-up

Joan has been contacted by phone several times in the 18 months since the May meeting. She consistently reports to the referring therapist that she feels secure, uplifted, confident, and "reempowered." In December 1991, she called for an appointment, but later canceled it when she realized that she actually had control of her anxiety and did not need to see anyone to help with it. Additionally, she has broken up her long-term (long-distance) relationship. She is now dating a man locally, and she reports that she is happy with this new love, and is in a supportive relationship for the first time.

# The Session

C: Client, Joan.
L: Stephen R. Lankton, M.S.W.

L: I'm from Pensacola and I flew in, and my ear hasn't cleared, so when you see me blowing this ear here. . . . It's not a permanent weird thing I do, just temporary for a couple of days after flying. And I know that your name is Joan, and I know a little bit about you because of the intake therapist's explanation. Her idea of sharing information with me that she had was to try to get a handle on anxiety, because you want to not have any anxiety.

C: Uh-huh.

L: So, it wasn't particularly enlightening. She filled out a checklist you might be interested in. . .

C: I know. Her checklist was a little tough. It was almost like I could check off everything, and then yet again. . . I. . . you know. . .

L: Oh, you're like me when you. . . if it takes hours to fill those things out.

C: And she'd say, "Now, don't take a long time. Just, you know, go through it."

L: I don't know. . . did I. . . are you. . . are you employed and taking out work to come here now?

C: Well, I'm on a part-time basis to do the medical. . .

L: Oh, as a Kelly. . . ?

C: No. I work at General Hospital for the outpatient psychiatric department with the psychiatrists.

L: Oh, oh that's right.

C: And I've just been out with hepatitis for five weeks.

L: Yeah, that's right. I recall some discussion from the therapist who referred you. Um, the checklist (Leary, 1957) is especially interesting. You might like to just glance at it, especially since it's not the kind of thing that would be doubtably good for you. On the circle, A is at the top. And it doesn't. . . it's not necessarily the truth, but it could have bearing. If it has bearing, then it's exceptionally useful. For most people in our age group, that aren't from California, use some or most of those words. It doesn't have things like "awesome" on there: You can't check "awesome" if you've got to, to know who you are. But the stuff above the horizontal middle line represents your self-report on how dominant and dominant behaviors you feel are available, and below it represents how many submissive behaviors you feel are available. You have checked mostly below the line, so the predominance of the evidence would convict you of being mostly submissive in your group of available behaviors to solve particular problems. So, if the world somehow suddenly or actively demands that you be. . . demonstrating dominant behaviors, then it would stand to reason that you'd get a little bit nervous because you don't think you have those in your toolbox. And that could account for some anxiety level right off the bat. Another thing that seems reasonable to consider that all of the things to the left of the vertical line have to do with basically moving away from people. And to the right of that, towards me, have to do with moving towards people. So, the one area, that upper quadrant from B, C, D, and E, is pretty much empty or totally empty compared to everything else, which says when it comes to being dominant and pushing people away, don't count on you to do it. And there's some times when the world requires that. You know, when I get those phone calls, when they want to sell me something I don't need. . .

C: Right.

L: And you have to listen to them, or, if, you have to say, "Look, don't call me up. I don't want to hear these phone calls." And that kind of conduct would be anxiety producing for somebody who doesn't think they have the ability to be dominant and push people away. So that kind of thing surely is also from time to time needed, I would think, especially in your job. And having children, as you do. . . how old is he?

C: I have. . . I have a son, 10.

L: He's the one that's with your husband and he's. . . 10? And when he comes to visit or you visit him, anything with children, you some time or another need to say, "I said, sit down, and I said don't talk right now." You know? That is dominant and disaffiliative behavior also. So now the next thing is. . . do you actually have those behaviors between P and F over there or something? It's possible that you do have some of those.

C: Well, I think I do.

L: In that your score when you criticized yourself may be different and may have kept you from checking such thing as "able to give orders" checked that particular one, thinking, "Well, I don't know" and you leave it blank. So *that* self-criticism may have been operating when you filled it out and could have kept that score lower.

C: Probably. I 'm pretty hard on myself. I mean. . . I. . . in my job I have to have a certain amount of control over a situation, and I do. . .

L: Yeah.

C: The only time that I really feel that I'm in control or that I have any self-confidence is when I'm at work.

L: Uh-huh. Oh. Uh-huh.

C: The only time I'm...behind a desk and there doing my job, and it's the only time that I feel that...

L: You have legitimate power.

C: Yeah, and then when my son comes down, the majority of the time I do feel...you know, I do feel in control of the situation. There's a period of when he first comes down that I don't...you know, adjusting, I guess, and then a few weeks before he gets ready to leave then I...

L: You realize you've kept from going out of control.

C: You know, I mean, because he's leaving, and I don't want him to leave, and it overpowers anything, you know, that...I mean my feelings overpower it, so I feel a bit insecure, you know, because I'm going to have say good-bye to him. Then I tend fall apart, I'm already preparing, you know, not deal with it very well.

L: Does that work out? Do you succeed 100 percent of the time? Do you then fall apart?

C: Yeah, well, the last two times I've been pretty good at, you know, keeping it together, which, you know, is kind of a breakthrough for me.

L: When does he come again?

C: He'll be here the end of June [four weeks].

L: Are you already preparing to fall apart, or do you wait...is there still, like a Labor Day weekend...or how do you do that? When do you know when to start? Do you need like a special amount of shopping time ahead to know...?

C: No, I just...

L: Only so many shopping days to get my falling apart together?

C: Right. Right. Well, at the point when he arrives, I'm nervous that, you know...we've been separated, so I'm apprehensive about where we are in our relationship as far as...

L: Yeah, really, that's a toughie.

C: Even though we talk on the phone almost every night. He's not a great conversationalist on the phone. "Hi, how are you? Well, what'd you do today?" "Nothing." You know, so he's not a great conversationalist on the phone, so the first week or so when he comes down...

L: Quite clearly, he could say more and isn't. So, that's kind of...

C: Yeah. So, the big adjustment, I think, is I seem to not have any control over the fact that as soon as...it's a week or two before he has to go back, we're preparing his plane ticket, we're making sure his clothes are ready, and, you know, we're trying to get in all our last minute things that we didn't do all summer that, you know, we didn't have a chance to do, or, you know, I'm thinking, "Did we do enough?" Did, you know, did we, did he, was this, you know, enough for him? That's when I start feeling the separation and that this is my last chance until next summer and...I don't know. I guess I don't feel like it's enough. I don't do enough, you know. Just about two weeks before he leaves, I start. And this past time now I threw myself and I just worked all the time and didn't really focus on it as much.

L: When he's down here, do you work part-time still?

C: I work full time, plus a second job. He goes to summer camp during the day, and I take care of an older couple at night, two or three nights a week, and they have a swimming pool and they live on a golf course, so he comes with me, and we swim and we hit golf balls, you know. All I do is cook their dinner basically, and make sure they're settled in for the night. And we all eat together, and, so that's done two or three nights now and he'll go to my sister-in-law's one of those nights, so that he'll be with kids.

L: That's a...that could be pretty nice, because it gives him a chance to see you interacting in the ways and modeling a "nice" person. Well, you're telling me you do. The words that got me, the words "fall apart," though is what stuck with me. That, you know, my older son used to go back to the real world after visiting. He's in Japan teaching right now, and a, so I've had some experience with the comings and goings of children you don't see very often. And, oh, and when I leave my father and understand his position, I can understand some of that questioning. But I wouldn't ask myself...I wouldn't say it's "falling apart," you know. I mean, that's the word that really struck oddly with me. I would think it might be maybe "sad"...

C: Well, I pretty much...of course, I pretty much [laughing] break down. I mean, you know, I...it just tears me up, you know. It doesn't seem...I mean, we've been doing this for years, and it doesn't seem to get...

L: You need to make peace with that somehow, with what your role is going to be with your son.

C: Right. Possibly, I just feel that, you know, he...something is being taken away from me every time he leaves.

L: When...I got a little bit of familiarization with your history. Your husband got custody like when he was three or four, something like that. So that would have been...what...he's 10, so seven years ago or so, seven or eight years ago. Well, gosh, you have...wait a minute, tell me about this...the goal here. The goal is to...I think that may be helpful to...The therapist who referred you mentioned that you'd been...that she had done a session with you where you put yourself in a trance and found that to be a possibility, and since I'm teaching professionals in hypnosis, it makes sense that that would be one of the tools we would use for your anxiety. And since people go into trance by basically putting themselves into a trance, the things that I say, if irrelevant, are totally irrelevant to the listener. So if I can be relevant, so much the better. And so talking about your son coming up in a month is very relevant, I'm sure, and if not now, will be soon. But I think I should hear some more from you about...what do you think...when did all this anxiety start? I don't really...I've gotten the words from someone else, but if I can see it through your eyes, if you could fill me in on what you'd like to accomplish or what you think we could accomplish or anything not to accomplish, whatever, anything.

C: Well, my anxiety is the only...you know, like I feel that things are, that things can end like that. You know, I have this on-the-edge feeling. With my history of my mother dying at an early age, that might...

L: You were three years of age?

C: Yeah, I was three; she was 30-...

L: She was 30?

C: ...She was 35...she was in her early 30s. And her sister the same thing. She also died in her early 30s.

L: And you were about 11 or something...12...when your grandmother died?

C: Yes. I just...

L: You had a lot of death that...of people that you would have been looking up to as a girl; it would have been bad if it had been a boy, but certainly as a girl...What would you do back in those days? Were you able to get comfort much from others to kind of help you brace it?

C: Not so much. When my grandmother died, my father had remarried, and, at that time, it's really hard for me to even remember what our relationship was like. I know it was okay, but they were both alcoholics. And my father is recovering now. And so it was more or less taking, we took, care of ourselves. I didn't have anyone that I really depended on.

L: Were you an only child?

C: No, I had three other...I had two brothers and a sister, a half-sister from my father's second marriage.

L: Are you the oldest...youngest, which?

C: I'm in the middle. I'm the youngest of the two...I'm younger than the two boys. And we were fairly close growing up. We did things together, hung out together.

L: Helped each other out and stuff?

C: Yeah, in that respect, we depended on each other.

L: So, when your mother died, you like all cried together and stuff?

C: Yeah? I don't remember that so much as my grandmother. I really don't remember my mother's death as much as I just remember the fact that

I saw her the day she died. I remember that. And then I don't remember the funeral. I don't remember...I really don't remember anything else.

L: You may not have understood what was going on.

C: I mean, it's hard for me to remember what she looked like. I've seen pictures, you know, I've looked at pictures and the other therapist and I have gone over things and I've tried to remember different things that we would do together, and I do remember a few things, but I can't visualize *her*. And my father never spoke about her after her death. After she died, he really didn't talk about it.

L: I can't, by the way, particularly picture my mother, and she died fairly recently. You don't know that that's probably a common thing, even if you had seen her for 10 more or 20 more years.

C: Yeah, but three was young, I mean...

L: Three is definitely the worst scenario because you really need to have her around when you're three.

C: And sometimes I think that I compare that to Brian, you know. I think that I'm not there, you know. And yet I am, but...sometimes I don't see a reason for me being there.

L: Well, you can if you want to be.

C: I know that I am, you know. Logically, I know that I'm there for him. I know that we have a good relationship. But I feel that I'm...I feel replaceable. I feel that, you know, there's not...he's settled in New Jersey with his father, you know. And it scares me that I feel that I don't have a purpose here. You know? Like I could die early, like my mother. And that'd be it, you know! And it's not really what I'd like to do. You know, I'd like to be around when he gets older and...but I have this fear of dying. I have this fear that there...if I fell off the face of the earth, you know, I think it would affect my son but...

L: Marginally? It would affect him marginally is all?

C: Yeah.

L: Have you ever asked him?

C: No.

L: Have you ever asked him about the divorce, how he feels about that?

C: We haven't really talked about it. As far as we have discussed, I had gone through some rough times, and we had decided that it was best if he lived with his father, because he would get the best that there was to offer, and that was the end of the discussion. Even though there's more that I want to know, you know.

L: He was how old?

C: He was almost four.

L: Yeah, that's a little tough. There's not much of a discussion really, you know.

C: But since then, you know, since then we haven't really...through the years we've had. . .you know, the amount of discussion was basically, you know, "You know that mommy loves you". . .

L: Is he pretty mature now or is he. . .for his age?

C: Yeah. I think he's pretty mature.

L: Maybe this is the time for a real quality discussion.

C: I think he's pretty mature for his age. . .very. . .

L: You could just bring it up. You say, "Have you ever wanted to talk about why we got divorced, why you went with your father, or anything like that?" "I don't know"—that's the proper answer for his age. "Well, in that case, I think yes. We're going to talk about it," you say. And then you say, "Let me tell you a few things that are on my mind." And he probably won't participate much. He'll probably just take it in and think about it. And you know what else? A good way to terminate that transaction. . .that two pages or five pages or whatever you have of mostly one-sided discussion with a kid that's saying. . .whose looking at you and saying nothing, and when you say, "Well, do you have any questions?" "No." The way to terminate it is. . .you can go on, and I should say, let's think about how to terminate it just a minute. Because if you terminate it by a look on your face that says, "Oh, God. I didn't think that could be worth going into," that's more information that he's taking in. Kids are especially, and in the unconscious part of all of us, as well, are really good for making sense of what just occurred onstage by what occurs as an offstage line. So, if, you know, you saw Julio Iglesias sing a wonderful bunch of numbers, or something, on stage in Las Vegas, and then they forgot to turn his mike off, and he walked offstage and said, "Now, I've got those damn people out. . .that damn job over with. . .and those stupid people out of there"—that would just ruin the whole performance. So, and if you heard the mike on and he said, "What a lovely audience," and "They made me feel so warm," and you'd think, "Gee, he really was a cool guy." So that offstage line helps you understand. So, likewise, when this whole thing is over and you say, "Any questions," and he says, "No," and you say, "Well, if you have any questions, you be sure to ask them, okay, Sweetheart?" And he goes, "Okay." Then you don't want to go, "Oh, Christ, I knew it wasn't going to do any good." You want to take what kind of dignity you want to portray to him. You don't want to show him, "Gee, I'm afraid he doesn't love me." You don't want to show him. . .you do want to show him, "I love him. That's all there is to it." "I love him," and that's what I want to talk about today. "I want to enhance him as a person," "some day when he grows up, he's going to be a better man because we had this talk, even if he doesn't say so now"—look on your face. That's the offstage line incident. Then you look at him and he goes, "Okay," then just kind of staring through him to see the man that he's going to become some day and be happy with his inner hapinesses.

C: Okay.

L: And then turn and go about your business, and that's that. And then, I'd say, you know, a couple of days later maybe, approach him again and say, "I know how hard it is sometimes to bring things up with someone you don't see very often, and I wonder if you've been thinking about what we said before and saying things with new grasp – and be, a, willing to talk about it. Because it is important that we investigate things when we have them. So now you can ask me anything you want." It might be a little more congruent when he says "okay" again. And then he probably still won't ask you anything, but a couple of years later he might. Or a couple of three, or four, or five . . . 10 years later, he might, you know, tell you, level with you, of the difference. You know, I've seen it a lot of times where the child who lives with the estranged – lived with one spouse and the one didn't see him – later said to that mother or to that father . . . Well, I had this one that was really very interesting, in fact, and I think says a lot of it . . . a couple of things that [faltering for a recollection], let's see, which one I wanted to . . . good feelings are on. Mostly, if the woman gets the custody and the man doesn't, and then there's remarriage and other children, and it's complicated like that, and a . . . So. And I'm thinking of this one that said . . . whose mother was an astrology buff. You know, in a big way! And that when the father finally knew that kid had liked him all along, was, he had [faltering for words] . . . This guy was like out of the house when the mother had been going off to Miami or something . . . and joined the Army . . . Gee, I can't remember the details exactly. He joined the Army, I believe. He went to the Army recruiter, and he told his mother he'd gone to a recruiter because he was thinking he wouldn't go to college or junior college and would go into the Army. She got out some kind of astrology deal to try to figure out whether this was a good decision to make on this day, and then he talked to his father that night, and when I saw his father (who told me that the boy had called him up and said that he had joined with a recruiter), and the father's response was favorable. And the father said, "Well, I'm glad you're making a decision, and I hope it'll work out for you." And he said, "Gee, Dad. That's such a refreshing thing. Mom just went to the astrology book and said this was a bad day for me to make decisions." You know, she's just always been . . . I don't remember the details . . . just some little subtle things that he finally shared. It's been years and years and years he'd been talking to this guy, had never given his father a clue that he had been listening to the mother gradually, just a little bit, bad-mouthing, just a little bit, nothing outstanding apparently. But the kid had been saving it up, and he finally concluded with that one extra straw on the camel's back that his dad was not so bad after all, and that his mother had been goofy all along. And that especially, that one did it. So that made me think, "Yeah, that's how it goes with different children." They might not really conclude at 14 or 16 or 17; they might wait until they're 21 to conclude. So, be aware that you may not find out until later. Well, anyway, so that's important. I wanted to get my two cents worth in, because I think when you say you want to know, if you had quality time, that sure as heck could help you do it. And it makes me think of something we could do to be useful later on, to have you reverse that in your mind so that you can see yourself pulling it off just a little bit more rather than being stuck a little. So you have a sense of being on the edge of being forgotten by him.

C: I guess. I can't...I don't know if...

L: If it's just that?

C: If I'm, you know, explaining it right. I feel really...

L: Disconnected?

C: Yeah, disconnected and...it's like when I'm at work, I'm so in control. I mean, I have a very responsible, I mean, totally stressed-out position, and I have a lot of people that depend on me, and I have no problem with it. As soon as I leave the office and I'm home, it's like, "Okay, now what do I do?" You know, I can't just live and work. I can't...you know...I'm finding that I don't...I just don't function that well in social functions. I have a lot of problems going to parties or being around a lot of people. I seem to call people more often than, you know, taking the chance of waiting 'till my phone rings. I...being out of work these past five weeks can really, like...totally showing me that, you know, I'm just existing here and...

L: Yeah, you paint a really vivid picture.

C: Yeah, and my anxiety, my panic attacks have come back the past four weeks. I've been off my medication for almost five weeks, well, it's five weeks now. I haven't been taking the medication. I have Xanax, but I don't...I've been hoarding them as I told my...because I can't afford to get my prescription refilled, so I don't take them that often. But I...

L: Well, I think you're painting a picture that's very articulate, and there's no reason that you should feel panicky, and that's something we ought to be able to help with. But, not withstanding that, the picture that you paint is very...one that I'm very sensitive to. You know, you talk like a person who is expressing a real American, I guess, or maybe it's a worldwide problem that leads a lot of people to get married for no good reason other than to avoid this fear and to have kids for no reason other than to avoid that emptiness and to get involved with drugs or something for no good reason other than for that sense of...

C: I've done it all—gotten married and got involved in drugs.

L: And who, given nothing to do, especially because of some other little problem, doesn't mean they're not employable because of their education or their race or something like that, or their sex, whatever has kept them from overcoming their geography or something has kept them from being employable, then they're a prime target to become victim of a mental health hierarchy that is all too willing to give them a label, give them drugs, and the more you participate in it, the more you feel more of what you wanted to avoid, sort of, because it...and...So, in a way, you're grappling with, a really, the "human condition," you know. And I don't know anyone that's particularly said, "Grappling with the human condition is a lovely piece of cake."

C: Right.

L: So, I don't know if that is supposed to be helpful advice, but, I bet, in a way it is supposed to be helpful advice, because if you think, "God, there's something wrong with me" versus "God the world is a little weird, but this is human condition." And rather than saying, "I'm weak because I'm feeling nervous and anxious and void," you could very well be thinking, "The world needs to not disenfranchise people because they're not married, childrearing consumers." The world needs to have a few places for people, not just married, childbearing consumers. And it's not. And I feel the result of that, and it kind of pisses me off, actually.

C: You're absolutely right.

L: So, it turns the focus on whether or not *you* should be the target of your disgust or this situation that we're all in. Because, as you talked, I heard myself in college going, "Gosh, if I drop out of college, I'm nothing." "If I don't get married, I'm nothing." And I know every man that I've... men don't generally talk about it, especially once they have power about them somehow. But that's why they seek it, I think, is to avoid a feeling that your having. Because, so there's a real strength and a real courage to continually face that difficulty. And every person I ever dated that came home from work and sat home alone felt that same anxiety. Now ...and what you're doing makes a great deal of sense...reaching out to other people and before they call you. The part that doesn't make sense is that you unfortunately still are willing to think, "Maybe there's something wrong with me, maybe that's it." So, while you kind of agree with what I'm saying, there's a part of you that sometimes says, well, okay, but "maybe it's me," and then when you get to that part, then you, then it all goes down the toilet, because you start feeling so crummy that you don't reach out and "people don't want to be around me."

C: Yeah, but I feel that sometimes I do it for the wrong...I mean, like men...my choice in men sucks. I mean, it's the pits. And every man that I've ever...

*L:* Stand-up comic. There's a role there for you.

*C:* I mean, it's just...and I do because I want to be close to someone, you know. And, you know...and they're so...it's usually men that have been friends of mine for years.

*L:* It seems like a good idea at the time.

*C:* And we've ended up in a relationship. And then it goes three or four weeks, and then the man starts to get a little panicky and then pushes me away. I mean, the only man that didn't push me away, he's already married, so he doesn't have to push me away. But, and that was probably the easiest relationship I've ever been in because, you know, there were no demands. It took care of our sexual, of my sexual, needs, and that was it. But for me to take...you know, like these guys are nice, but they're not really for me. But yet because the way we get close and, you know, see each other and hang out and know each other, I didn't have to prove myself...you know, I was already accepted, but it would only go so far. It would go for three or four weeks, and then it would be, like, well, we've got to cool it, or I'm getting a little nervous, or I can't make a commitment. Me, I don't want a commitment, just be there, you know, as far as just...And I think, "God," you know...I mean, it's not like...I do it to replace the fact that I don't have my son in my life and I need someone to care for. I need someone to care for me. But why do I need that? Why can't I just be on my own and not depend on, you know, falling into bed with someone? You know, that's another concern. I don't want to have to do that because it's an icky feeling afterwards, you know.

*L:* Yeah, maturing can take all the fun out of all those crummy things.

*C:* [Laughing] I know. It...but I know why I do that. I know that, you know, I'm easy...not "easy" easy...I'm an easy mark.

*L:* Yes, I'll erase that comment from your record. Strike it!

*C:* I'm a easy mark. I have a lot of friends that are men that like me, and that we get along, and I make them feel good, you know, so then it turns out, you know, we've spent an evening together, we go out to dinner or something, and we end up in a relationship, you know, and it was easy [snaps her fingers]...you know, just happened, you know, and it felt good.

*L:* Yeah.

*C:* But then, you know, it either has to stop there or, you know, I want more than that. You know, I...

*L:* Yeah. You say that now, but as you're saying that at 11:30 on Friday night, you're not remembering that you're going to be saying that now. As your graph over here says, when it comes around to making demands on other people, which would be this area [pointing to the ICL graph], that it's not the first tool you grasp onto.

C: Right.

L: From your toolbox.

C: I think it all the time. You know, I can say, okay, you know . . . And I am . . . I can be forward as far as, you know, like if I want to see someone, it doesn't bother me to call him up and say, you know, "What are you doing?" or "I'd like to see you," or "Are you free?" or "I can use some company." And I've done that.

L: So, okay. Well, tell me this then. Maybe this is . . . this sounds like you're . . . you're very thoughtful and articulate and courageous, and you know what else you are very good at that you don't know about? Is trying to frame this entire matter of your life and your anxiety and dilemma in a, . . . what's the right word for this? . . . kind of an intellectually accurate way rather than an easy way. An easy way would be to say, oh, I'm a . . . something with a label . . . "I'm a cyclothemic," or "I'm a schizophrenic," or "I'm a" . . . whatever you are in somebody's mind from a textbook or something, which would be the easy way out. Or I just can't or whatever you . . . There's a lot of easy outs you could take that you've not taken. And perhaps you took easy outs in the past and you're remembering things that were easy outs that you took, but you sound very willing to be a fighter.

C: Sometimes I think I'm waiting for this . . . I'm waiting to have the nervous breakdown I should have had when my son was given to his father. You know, I never . . .

L: Well, now's a good time. I've got 45 minutes. Perhaps . . .

C: I never [laughing] . . . it's true that I . . . that's when I say, you know, I . . . Sometimes I feel like I'm ready . . . I'm at that point, you know, when I get into a depressed point. But I don't allow that to happen. And I never have allowed that to happen from the time that he was . . .

L: Well, you're off work now. You know that commercial that says you haven't got time for the pain? Well, you've got time. Go ahead and have it.

C: You know, I could have gone into a hospital, and then I thought, no, that would look worse on my records, you know, back then when he was taken away from me, so that I fought, you know, and . . .

L: Why do you think you have to have a nervous breakdown?

C: No, I mean sometimes when I . . .

L: To be complete? It's sort of like, you know . . .

C: No, it's like, let me get it over with, and then I'll be fine for the rest of my life.

L: Yeah, right. Where do you get this idea that there's a nervous breakdown in the box that has to be? It doesn't say that in the instruction manual. Okay, lose child, go home, have a nervous breakdown, pick up parts, put them in the box.

C: Well, I think, you know, I'm "recovering" too from drugs and alcohol, and I have had a couple setbacks in the past year and one-half.

L: But you need to answer that question. Where do you get the idea... that's the predominant thing that keeps coming around. Why does it? Where do you get the impression that that's part of the deal?

C: I, you know, I don't know. I think it's just... you're right. It's just in my head where I feel like I just want to take a break from feeling everything.

L: That's cool to take a break, but having a nervous breakdown isn't an especially good break... Bimini is a much better idea. Bahamas is good.

C: Right. Well, then I can deal with that. I can deal with that. No, I mean, there are times when I'm tired. You know, where I just want to shut everything off, but I know that I can't do that. You know, I can't. You know, I have to function, I have to be there. You know, I can't... I used to escape and get high and stoned, and, you know, not care, and then realize the next morning that those things are there, and are still going to be there. You know... am I making any sense?

L: You're making a lot of sense, except that you skip past the part where you don't have an explanation and you think you've answered that for yourself. But you didn't. And it seems like you should, really.

C: Answer myself about why I deserve a nervous breakdown?

L: Well, yeah. Why do you think it has to be that?

C: I mean, it's not that I think it has to, but sometimes I feel... Like Mother's Day. Mother's Day was really rough on me, and I felt... sometimes I feel like I'm fighting it.

L: Oh, you've equated, yeah, you're holding on because you really want to let go, and if you do let go, that will be bad. What is this holding-on/letting-go thing? Why does that seem like such a fight?

C: I don't know. It is, though. It is a fight.

L: Well, you know, if you think of it as one and you're close to it, you get frightened, and maybe it's not a fight at all, and you just thought it was. So you're kind of like avoiding it, and the closer you get, the more you avoid it, and it really is a struggle. Maybe it's not such a bad deal after all. After all, everything else you do seems to be handled with a great deal of... especially, I think the key word here is your ability to articulate it so well. When you can articulate all these little nuances of your experiences as wonderfully as you do, it's impossible for a person like that to get lost in the... inner experience. I mean, you have a whole bunch of things to hang on to when you're having these experiences.

C: But it's so negative. Mother's Day. Mother's Day should be a positive day for me. I mean, I'm the mother of a beautiful son and I was depressed Mother's Day. I was, you know... and I fight with myself, saying, you know, try... why...

L: And you practice so very much feeling proud and happy. I'll just bet.

When was the last time that you practiced feeling proud and happy?

C: I can't remember [laughing].

L: Well, then, how in the hell do you expect to be an expert as the clock turns midnight and not even do what you practiced? I have a brother-in-law who's an expert classical guitarist, and at midnight he could play classical guitar when the clock turned to "Classical Guitarist Day" (I think that there probably is one on the calendar somewhere). And... But he practices all the time at that. So, I was thinking you probably must have practiced being proud and happy if you thought you were just going to "kick it in" at midnight. You don't practice that? Oh, God, you're as bad as my seven-year-old.

C: In fact, I go up to people, begging them to ask me about my son so I can brag about him, you know, and that doesn't happen too often.

L: You have to kind of force that on them a lot of times. There's home movies.

C: I know. There's pictures. I have them all over the place. Do you want to... by any chance, do you want to see any pictures?

L: Let me see... got one?

C: Now I don't...

L: Good practicing! I'm really convinced now.

C: No, I took them out. When I got out of the hospital, I took them out of my frame and I have them in another purse. My purse was stolen with all of my pictures from the time he was four years old until the time he was 10. And I had them in a thing that you just flip over. So, I have not had those replaced.

L: I threw my wallet away in an Ace Hardware bag once. When I came home, I put my wallet in, and I tossed it out with all my... a whole bunch of my pictures like that too.

C: That's the only thing that broke me up about having the purse stolen was from... every year from the time he was three...

L: Maybe you can get copies from your ex-husband?

C: Yeah, I'm working on replacing them, going through some old pictures that I have.

L: Well, speaking of pictures, close your eyes for just a minute and see if you can picture that series of photographs of him from three to recently (or whatever that group was that was missing), and while you're picturing them, I'm going to be watching your face and giving you a little mental grade here. The truth of the matter is, I'm wondering how you feel that feeling of pride that you said you never practiced feeling. So, scanning that series of pictures, pick up any feeling of pride or happiness that you have on seeing his beautiful development. Because that's what those pictures are for, aren't they? They're sort of like anchors to having located, "Oh God, he's cool," and pick up a good feeling... and a fantasy has some...and pick up a good feeling. Of course, good feelings might have some smile attached. Some good feelings might have some sort of, like, laughter attached. Some good feelings might have tenderness attached. So they're all of the same theme, but the whole group of it is really your pride in being the mother. When you scan that, can you feel a feeling of change as you do? That's practicing! It's working! You're doing a lot of heavy swallowing sometimes. You're kind of doing a little fidgeting. Is there something else going on?

C: No. He just grows up so fast.

L: I tell you what. While you've got your eyes closed and you're picturing that, let's put that aside for just a second here, so you can come back to it later if you want. But go, picture yourself growing up from, let's say, you've got a model of mental imagination just warmed up to seeing a child get bigger and bigger. Can you take a picture of yourself, and as you go back in the other direction, and get smaller and smaller? And go back to watching yourself at three or four? You're sort of succeeding at it, I take it?

C: Uh-huh.

L: For just a moment, go back to the picture. Come back up to a picture of the present of yourself, let's say, come back up the line to practice that imagination again. And come back to the series of pictures of your son and scan through those again. You may notice by juxtaposition your feelings switch. I'm not certain whether it did or not. Okay, this time when you scan the pictures of your son, hold onto that good feeling. In fact, maybe you should uncross your legs so that you can relax a little bit more deeply. And a...The more you relax, the more there is a capability of letting your imagination drive your feeling state. The more tense you are, the more your legs are crossed or something, the more you're feeling state is stabilized by your body position, so get yourself to the degree necessary and possible to really make solid sense of that good feeling of yourself while you're feeling that joy and awareness— that parents have as times change, an' moments of pride and joy. Now you have a group of those built up, is that correct? Okay, maybe you could hold your wrist or something as a way of kind of signaling yourself that you're gonna hold on to those feelings, and now let's go back to that other series. Hold onto that feeling of being a...(I don't want to make the wrong word, but whatever the right word is for) being a mother who's got pride and happiness and joy and so on. Hold onto that feeling and skip back along the series of pictures of yourself as an increasingly younger girl, but hold onto those same feelings of, not the negative-ish feelings removed, but rather let the good feelings be a sense of feeling you've had as you make a picture of yourself as younger and younger.

So you can picture that feeling of yourself even as a three-year-old Joan, with a feeling of a caring mother in your heart, I guess you might say, and while you're seeing yourself while you're feeling a little piece of the doubt. And let me know what's happening. How about if you let your unconscious hold onto that feeling of being a caring mother and concerned, proud mother while you let your conscious mind keep picturing that picture of a three-year-old Joan or a three or four year-old Joan. And from time to time, it might flip to where your conscious mind is aware of your being a loving mother while your unconscious is holding onto a sense that you're imaging that three- or four-year-old inside. And while you're keeping that relationship, imagine talking to that little three-year-old, from the future, and telling her, "Sweetheart, I care about you and I love you. We can help one another in a very useful way in feelings. Just communicate with me a little bit and it will be okay." And ask her to nod her head if that's okay. And tell her that you're from her future, that it's probably confusing for her about all the stuff that's going on, and that you understand it much better now than she would back in those days and you'd be glad to answer any questions for her. But most of all, you want her to know that you love her and that you care about her and you're proud. You know how to be a proud mother who cares about a child. And that even though it may have sort of occurred to her that she was never going to know how proud mothers felt about a child, that you are a proud mother, feeling that way about her right now. And that you've reviewed pictures of her growing up and felt like a proud mother: a mother who has sometimes felt joy, a mother who has sometimes felt sadness and overall compassion about how, good, quickly she's going to grow up. And the two of you can do a favor for one another if she's willing. First of all, ask her to know that. . . to give you that head nod again, if she realizes that you feel like a proud mother towards her and a loving mother towards her. And ask her to memorize that because you want her to take that sense with her as she grows up, so that she gets to know what it's like to have a mother who cares about her and follows her progress and provides continuity of love and amazement as a child grows. And then here's the deal. Tell her that you understand as an adult what she doesn't quite yet get, in your own words. I don't need to tell you, but I might give you some words that you might want to modify. But take my words and change them so they fit for you as a person. Tell her that she could provide for you something and you could provide for her something— make a little trade that you each benefit from, if that would be okay. Here's what it is. You be the mother for her who's proud and amazed and sad and tender and happy and loving and caring, if she can be the little girl for you to provide continuity that you need on the side of that equation. And ask if that would be all right, if she would put you in touch with the sadnesses and happinesses and joys of a little girl in your quest for the amazement that a little girl has. In trade, for her the protection and the love and caring that you could provide her as a grown woman and surrogate mother. Ask her if that would be a good trade that she would be willing to do. It seems like it would be fun for her. And signal you somehow with a head nod or words inside your head that she'd like that from you—she'd like that from somebody. [Long pause] Imagine making a deal or a trade of some kind happen when you feel something in your heart or feel something in your stomach that indicates she's signaling you that she has a need for that mother so that she can use that feeling in the future to let your conscious mind be alert to the fact that your unconscious is having a need of some kind for your end of the bargain in this. And whenever you have that sense that there's no purpose or point in your being around, unless the child needs you to be, that you need to hear from her that she's got some need, that she appreciates that, and maybe her idea, her age, will come to your conscious mind as a signal from her to you that your unconscious is wishing to once again establish that contact. And rehearse making that trade so that you can have these resources available at those times in the next few days and weeks and years to come. And perhaps you'll even be able to help that little girl grow up more confidently, more happily. And I guess you ought to ask her if she thinks she would grow up to become more happy if she had a mother like you to care about her. And if that's the case, then I think you should go ahead and tell that there's another part of the secret, which is that you'd be a lot happier too if you knew somebody continually needed you and was happy that you were happy to be needed. And the two of you could exchange that happiness with each other. And have each other to be around for one another. And if that's the case, then maybe you can even hear her giggle. That'd be pretty nice to hear her giggle again. I know that when my little girl giggles, it's about the happiest sound I've ever heard. My little boy giggles okay, but my little girl giggles so much better. And let the sound of that little girl that you love, and once were and still are, just echo and vibrate throughout your bones. Let the giggle replace the vibration of anxiety, in fact. Ask her if it would be okay with her if you used her giggle to replace that sense of anxiety. If she wouldn't feel too put upon if you use it in that way, because you sure could use it. I asked my little girl once when I was going on a trip if it would be okay, whenever I started to feel sad and lonely, if I remembered her giggle and helped the giggle to come instead of the tears, and she said, "it would make me as proud as the day I got my DPT shot, Daddy." And then watch yourself watching her, if you can. It's a very difficult thing to do, but I think the

Joan sitting up there on the couch is capable of picturing the Joan sitting on a couch who's, in the picture, is, in turn, picturing that little girl. And watch that relationship between that mother and that child. Review that agreement we just made and make sure it fits your sense of dignity as a person and your values, and add anything to it you'd like to have. It might look like a very appropriate couple when you see them together. And it might just be that things become happy for you guys, too. And it might mean that your unconscious can make some connections to answer some questions that your conscious mind may be flirting with, and thinking about for years, as you watch the two of them be mother and child together. Use it as a meditation to go into self-hypnosis as deeply as necessary to let ideas come to your mind to answer questions that are difficult to articulate and to ask, and more difficult to be answered, because you're. . .you don't need to fully understand answers that you get in order to appreciate them. And if the picture is somehow aesthetically balanced for you at a point, so that it brings you a feeling of more completeness and more satisfaction.

And as you watch the picture of the grown-up Joan watching the little Joan, not just watching, but trading those experiences with her and holding her hand, let your mind tune out these other distractions unless the sounds of those children simply help you realize the energy that the child can bring you. They are of no concern to you. Just relax increasingly. And the more relaxed you become, the more deeply you go into trance, so that you make it possible for. . .a depth of concentration and alertness to your own experience, to help that learning that you're picturing in your mind continue on, connecting the part of you where the questions are. I could count systematically so that it will help you recognize the important of systematic relaxation added in between. Maybe you could notice the increase in the depth or deepening of relaxation. Ten, nine, eight, seven. And while I'm doing that, why not alternate that picture of the grown-up Joan holding that little three-year-old or four-year-old. Seven. Just a little bit more relaxed so that by the time you reach "one". . .And in the picture now there is some trust established, an understanding of your relationship and continuity will exist over the years, . . . Six, five, four. . . . tell her you're willing to talk with her about her mother's going away. Three. That you've already thought that through how to discuss that with the child. And you just wonder if she's got any more sadnesses about it or confusion about it. And you just want to hold her if she's sad and tell her that you'll be right there for her. Three. Two. One. And watch her move toward you, depend upon you as you hold her head and brush her hair, hold her real close. Tell her you understand how not understanding really hurts. That is, in fact, Joan, I think mostly all that a parent can say — is that it's hard for you and I understand. And you're still going to grow up to be a wonderful person and a beautiful child, and I love you. And it's so sad that your mom is not gonna get to see the beautiful person you're gonna grow up to become. And you might see that grown-up Joan demonstrate crying to the child as you sit there relaxed with the depth of trance necessary to let some answers reconnect to your unconscious, come to an understanding of what your conscious mind can construct in conjunction with your unconscious memories like that as you watch that grown-up Joan and the young Joan share that relationship of mother and daughter. Then lead her to four and move her to the five. And give her a chance to repeat those same questions again, and any of the other questions as that one eventually becomes answered for her. And make sure you tell her from time to time, so that you know it's important that she didn't get to hear, "I'm so sorry your mother couldn't have lived to see what a neat thing it is that you lost these teeth. I'm so sorry. Your mother would have been so proud to have seen you in that first little prom curtsy dress. Gosh, your mother would have been proud to see you at that first prom. And eventually just hearing that "I'm proud of you for riding the bicycle around the block" will come through to that little girl. She really knows that "someone loved" part is real important. And still, over the years, I think, from time to time, the proper thing is to say it again—from time to time. You know, it occurs to me again that, "I was so proud to see you again with that report card." "You bringing a lot of joy in the world." And while you may have forgotten about this in your mothering, since I'm a grown-up, I know that your mother got deprived of a lot of joy in seeing you, and I'm glad you're sharing it with me. Because that's what you can do for me. And you might remind her of the deal that you made. You'll provide that caring and that attention and that loving, that nurturing and that respect that's important for her. And in trade you'd need something that she's got that would be easy for her, if you could just have her share that need to know somebody really enjoys what she did. It's so nice to be able to light the face of someone else with a smile when you giggle as a little girl. When you come home with a report card that you're proud of. And when you learn to ride your tricycle around the block at a younger age than your brother did. And when you lived through the DPT shot. And when you made that special mud pie and pretended it was really something to eat. I think you have a lot of "that's really cool I'd say"s to do and a lot of "thank you—I'm really proud of myself"s to share. So watch the little girl say it. Watch the grown-up you say it. There's so many instances at six or seven and back sometime as far as you can imagine imagining. And as close as the depth of your grandmother to you when she begins to get to know your advantage. Take all the time you need, because being a mother is a lifetime job and being a father is a lifetime job.

And I'll just bet the spirit, and ghost, of your mother is here somewhere and would be very happy and very pleased indeed to know that you hit upon this idea. And I'll bet her soul rests a lot more easily realizing that fine little girl has someone who really needs a little girl, and is able to appreciate all the wonderful things that she was unable to demonstrate appreciation for due to her early death.

I don't know whether if anyone should believe it or not, but one of my clients told me a remarkable story. When he was in trance concentrating, he'd gone into trance thinking about a piece of old antique furniture that was from the house where his father had lived during his life—when he moved out of the house where his father had lived when he was a boy. It was refinished and actually from the house. And he concentrated on that as a way of going into a trance, as you do with common things that *you're* working on now. And when he came out of trance, he said, "You know, when you talked about seeing myself over there at a distance, it was easy for me because of something I've thought about a lot when I was little. And I was in bed one day, and I thought I was having a nightmare or something, and I saw this man standing at the foot of my bed all dressed in work clothes and a beard, like he'd been at a job all day long working on the railroad. And I shouted and my father came into the room and said, 'What is it?' and I described it. And something odd about my father's face when I described that man to him. He looked under the bed and tried to convince me there was nothing there: "Go to sleep, Sweetheart." But then, for some reason, he took me into his room, and we had no sooner gotten there, to the bedroom, when all of a sudden the huge plaster ceiling in that old house collapsed. It broke the bed and demolished the contents of the room, and I surely we would have been injured, if not killed, by that falling ceiling. And the next day when we woke up and surveyed the damage, my father had the same mysterious look on his face and he said, "I want to show you something." And he went up and took me into the attic where I'd never been before. All those memories up in the attic that I'd never seen. My father navigated through them over to an old chest. And he dusted the chest off and opened it up. The chest I'd never been in and never seen before. And at the bottom of the stack of all kinds of papers wrapped in leather and cloth, he pulled out an old photograph, and he blew the dust off of it, and he went downstairs to show it to me in the light. And I pointed to the second man from the right, and I said, "That's the guy I saw come into the bedroom, Daddy." And my dad started crying and said, "That's my father. He died when I was three." And he said, "Isn't that a strange story? I don't believe in ghost stories, but that was the very man I saw standing in the room in my imagination."

I didn't know what to say. And I thought, "Well, I've heard stories about how, sometimes, the whole field of ghost stories, is that the ghost doesn't rest because of unfinished business or something. While I never believed it much, maybe it helped your father's father finally rest because he was able to save a child's life—A child, that by saving the life of his only son's child, he finally had satisfied that need that was interrupted when he was unable to be a father to his own son." And I offered that to him as a suggestion and analogy. Maybe he did. And then, by that action, somehow being able to free his spirit and die in peace. And my client just looked at me like I was nuts and said, "I don't believe in ghosts." I wish I'd never mentioned it, because I don't particularly believe in ghosts either, but that story kind of answers a weird question. Maybe, in some way, that spirit of your mother has been satisfied in realizing you hit upon a way that frees *her* now to rest in peace knowing that the little girl that she abandoned can bring a smile to the face of her mother, who really needs a smile brought to her face by a child on a regular basis; whose needs to find a child have found one who needs a mother. And they both agreed to it and spend a great deal of time beginning the process of mothering, daughtering, sharing, needing, nurturing, and giggling. And while you're picturing those various ages of Joan and the little girl, why not picture Joan in the summer of 1991 as a grown-up, beginning to feel anxious and asking the little girl to help her remember what giggling sounds like? So that she finds out that when she's just about got anxious, her giggling little girl replays the game again. So that that little girl knows that she really is valuable to the grown-up, too.

What a nice way to fall apart with people. A lot of times my little girl has lost the control by giggling. And she gets me giggling so hard that we start giggling with the fact that we're giggling. That happened just a couple of days ago when I was trying to explain something to her, and I remembered something else in the middle of my explanation and turned to her and pointed my finger and said, "Whoa, whoa!" interrupting my former explanation—totally different behavior and suddenly pointing the forepaw out and my little girl just thought that was so funny, she knew exactly what had happened. And she started giggling that I did that, and I started giggling that she realized that. And that it was funny. And we sat there looking at each other's faces and giggled, tried to wipe the tears of giggle from our faces. Which caused us to giggle harder. So picture those two face-to-face giggling, and then step into the picture and be inches away from that little Joan's face, as she giggles watching your face giggling back. And know the joy of being a mother. Little Joan learning from the experience: Her giggles are very valuable, very appreciated. It's not the kind of thing that you can ever put into words that make sense until you get as old as we are and can understand parenting. But it does that child so much good to know that she was able to bring such joy to an adult. And maybe that's the greatest service we can provide to those children: to let them know that "You're valuable. It's important that you're here." And she'll never question when she grows up whether or not it's important that you feel valued. Because her very spirit and soul have made an impression that's important to an adult, and appreciated, and irreplaceable. No one else except that child did that—that laughter happened that time. My little girl knows she's valuable to me because I enjoy her. And I imagine that children are aware of all the crummy stuff they see across the face of moms and dads throughout the years. And they know the value of that smile and that joy and compared to that look of "I can't get the check-book to balance,". . . "I forgot to take out the garbage out again." By comparison, the look of that smile tells the child right away without question, "My laugh is valuable." A lot better than the look of that checkbook or garbage. "I did that, simply from my spirit." Of course, a child doesn't think that consciously, but your unconscious thinks it, and your unconscious knows it, and it's part of your makeup. And it stays with you forever.

And you might let some knowledge from that little girl also be helpful to you as a grown woman. Watch Joan interacting with her, and eventually think about how you interacted with your son during the summer when you have a certain talk with him. Know how his mother will find it. And then maybe some wisdom from that little girl, that will help you orchestrate that discussion in the most meaningful way for everyone involved. The little Joan, the young boy, and grown-up you. So, if you want to, take a moment to rehearse that discussion and what you might say, and especially how you might feel: proud of yourself for doing it; knowing that you're helping him know that he is making a valuable contribution that's important to you. And pay special attention to that moment of when you go offstage and make these final offstage comments.

I think that smile you've had on your face that you've learned from the little girl you once were would be a perfect transaction to show. And maybe you ought to go back and tell that little child that gave you that smile "someday when you talk to another little boy who has been separated from his mother, you're gonna use her smile, the smile you got from her, and you just wanted her to know how valuable it was, how very valuable it's going to be someday. And you just wanted her to know that. That you're glad to have that opportunity to tell her."

And, Joan, put all of these ideas in a safe place so they can continue to be nurtured and loved and grown and used. As you are, in the evening, needing something to do, I think you should practice. Practice being a pride-filled person in this way. It's so obvious the things parents should be with their children. Whether you had parents or not who raised you, they invariably forget to teach this to their children. And I'm glad you hit upon it, so you can use it with yourself again and again to develop the kinds of good feelings that often go unrehearsed and unpracticed.

And there's no reason to have a beautiful boy if you can't have some of the good feelings of connection and joy. And I just know that having the tools placed in your hand, you'll use them. So take your time for the next couple of minutes to think about the various ways in which you can find avenues back to these ideas. And simultaneously think ahead to times when you'll be sleeping at night and dreaming, or awake, purposely and sit down and meditate, if you want to, and use self-hypnosis, or you can just dream about them, night dreams or day-dreams. Or when you're alone and want to, just think about it in some way again. Reinstall, replace, wipe out any feelings of unpleasantness that you're having. Think about the times you're going to want to use these feelings, and let your unconscious find various avenues to bring them to mind in the future; or let your unconscious think ahead to when you're going to want to use these conscious memories, these experiences, in the future, to vividly learn, at the very first sign of dread and anxiety, detachment in living, in the next few weeks and all the years to come — and the holidays, the birthdays, the Mother's Days, the New Year's Days, the After Johnny Carson's Over Days, the "no one called me back on the telephone again" days. And look forward to any improvements you can make through repeated practice. And I'll count forward from one to 10 so that you can reorient yourself to the count, to the room and light and surroundings. I'd like to conclude that, in preparation, you continue what you began here in a way that's appropriate for you to keep doing to bring these ideas to a full and beneficial conclusion over the next few decades to come. One. Two. Three. Four. Five. And it would be a good thing to reorient your sensory apparatus to the room and sounds. Six. Seven. And your elongated muscles. Eight. And fine motor movements come back. Nine. Ten. Hi.

C: Hi.

L: How long of a time do you think you had your eyes closed?

C: About 10 or 15 minutes.

L: So, you'd be surprised to find out that it's 10 minutes after 11:00.

C: That was a long time.

L: It must have been about. . . a little over an hour, maybe close to an hour and 15, 20 minutes.

C: At first I thought I wasn't going to. . . when you were counting and I was trying to come. . .and I thought that I was going to stay right there. I felt like I was going to stay there.

L: Well, I guess you're going to go practice that. I guess that's your sign that there was some useful material that you want to practice.

C: Oh, yeah. Oh, yeah. God!

L: Well, any other comments or questions for me?

C: I think, I mean I feel pretty good right now. You know, I feel really good. Like I skipped something here. Like the first part of the session. I mean, I feel like. . .I feel pretty good. I think I'm certainly going to practice that, you know. Because in the beginning, I felt really sad and depressed, actually.

L: In the past, you used to feel depressed, huh?

C: And now I seem to. . .I don't know. I'm not focusing on that.

L: Yeah, you know what? It's that you haven't practiced enough to have as good a verbal articulation of feeling good that you are trying to communicate, isn't it? There's a void between your ability to articulate well and what you've said before, and now you've got a lot to articulate and you'll have to go get a dictionary and look up the words that are synonymous.

C: It's like. . .how do I express this feeling?

L: You need a thesaurus. Yeah, right. I have a dictionary on my computer, which is really neat, really handy. It's. . .it puts up. . .if you highlight a word and the definition that's on the screen, it'll look up the word immediately—it tracks. . .you know how you look up and a word and it says "dignity" and dignity means dah-dah-dah-dah-dah and noble. And you go. . .noble. . .hum. . .I wonder what actually what "noble" means. And now you've got to look up "noble," and then you get distracted because you've hit upon the word "Alfred Nobel" and you go "I want to know about Alfred Nobel," and you forget what you were searching, you know. So the thing is now it's instant, so it's so neat to be able to skip from one word to another and track down words like "courteous" and "polite" and "proud" and "happy" and "noble" and "dignity," and so on, and read what each of them means compared to the others. It's really very handy to do that. I was doing it the other day. . .there was someone on the telephone actually. We had a long-distance phone call. It started with some word like. . .we wondered if "redneck" was in the dictionary or "yokel," and what "yokel" meant compared to. . .I called him a "yokel," he said, "I'm a 'redneck,' " and I looked it up. It turns out that "yokel" means you have to be kind of a clown about it.

C: Oh, "he's a local yokel."

L: Yeah. And so he's always making visual ideograms, like, "well, it's just like a lame duck splashes in the water." And I said, "You know, you must be a yokel to have all these little phrases," and he said, "I'm not a yokel," so we started looking up. And we ended up looking up words like "dignity" once we started with words like "yokel" and "redneck," we're looking up "dignity" and... what was the other one that was right up there that turned out to be interesting that we had gotten to? We were tracking down "courteous" and "polite" and also...oh, there were other words like "well-bred" and "well-mannered" and...I'll have to think about it a little bit more, but it was odd that we had gone from this one set that was relatively negative and gone all the way to this other one, and I realized how...it was a good exercise in learning to articulate things that you usually don't. The difference between "polite" and "courteous"—"courteous" is a warm regard for the dignity of others. Sounds good, doesn't it.

C: Yeah. Sounds nice.

L: Well, maybe we should say good-bye, and shall I send the other therapist back in? I guess she said she'd come.

C: Yeah.

L: Well, it was very nice meeting you. I'm glad that you're having such a nice time.

C: Well, it was very nice meeting you. Thank you so much for your time and...I mean, it was really good, you know. And I hope that I can do...you know, do it myself and so...I think I can.

L: Yeah. Do you have a sense that you can?

C: I think I can.

L: Well, I think you'll do it.

C: I feel I'll be able to.

L: Well, that's great.

C: So, you're heading back then.

L: Yeah, tonight I will, if those thunderstorms don't stop me.

C: Thanks a lot. Bye-bye.

## References

Leary, T. (1957). *Interpersonal diagnosis of personality: A functional theory and methodology for personality evaluation.* New York: Ronald Press.

# Back to the Future: Cocreating a Different Life Story

## William J. Matthews, Ph.D.

*In this case analysis the work of Lankton with Joan is considered from the Ericksonian principles of (1) an emphasis on the positive strengths of the client, (2) the use of the developmental life cycle to normalize behavior, (3) a solution orientation, (4) the use of hypnosis to build new associations, and (5) the use of the therapist self with humor in support of a general goal of attaining enjoyment in living. Specifically, Lankton is seen as helping the client to reparent herself as a child in order to develop positive resources to enjoy her relationship with her adolescent son and others in her social network. Testing the efficacy of the work in session and the use of posthypnotic suggestions are discussed.*

As a child, I remember reading H. G. Wells' *Time Machine* and being totally fascinated with the idea of time travel. Once, when my father punished me by sending me to my room for some violation (no doubt completely unwarranted), I yelled out to him that when time travel became a reality, I would go back in time to when he was a small boy and teach him a lesson or two. Apart from the obvious Freudian-oedipal possibilities, the notion of traveling back and forth in time as one might travel from place to place is intriguing. To see and experience various important historical events and persons would be an amazing experience. In reviewing a particular historical event, one could have an entirely different understanding of the meaning and impact of that event on present-day experience. In my view, the essence of the present case is Lankton's use of "time travel" to coconstruct with Joan a different, more useful story.

## Ericksonian Principles

There were a number of key Ericksonian principles permeating

Address correspondence to William J. Matthews, Ph.D., 22 Foxglove Lane, Amherst, MA 01002.

Lankton's work with Joan, which provided a guideline in my analysis of it. These principles are (1) emphasizing positive strengths, abilities, and skills versus a pathology-oriented focus on weaknesses or failures; (2) emphasizing a predictable developmental life cycle where difficulties in living are expected to occur; which then leads to (3) using a solution-focused/future-oriented approach to change versus a problem-focused/ historical orientation; (4) employing indirect and direct suggestions, utilizing client presentation, and creating a useful split between conscious and unconscious ways of knowing; and finally (5) using humor and stressing the importance of enjoyment in living.

## The Case Analysis

### Assessment as Intervention

In the initial phase of the interview, from my perspective, Lankton seeks to develop rapport with Joan, to assess her strengths, and to normalize her concerns as much as possible. This creates a positive expectancy for change. Importantly, the assessment process is not separate from the intervention and solution focus of this approach. Throughout the session, Lankton attempts to assess various strengths and to offer, either directly or indirectly, alternative meanings of her experience. There is a smooth flow from assessment, to intervention, to evaluation of the intervention, and back to assessment across the session. For example, he explains the meaning of her responses to the Interpersonal Checklist (ICL), rather than withholding the information. Joan states that the ICL was difficult for her, implying a self-critical assessment. Lankton simply states, "Oh, you're like me, it takes hours to fill those things out." Within the initial minutes of the session, Lankton, for me, has begun to create a context for change. He normalizes her concerns, and suggests that he and she are alike in some ways.

In explaining the ICL, he suggests the importance and value of being able to show dominant behaviors. Again in this initial part of the session, Lankton will make a clear didactic statement about an issue such as the importance of dominant behaviors, and then present a simple anecdote emphasizing the value of dominant behaviors, as in dealing with tele-marketers. Joan readily agrees to the value of such skills in that instance. Lankton, having attained her agreement about managing telemarketers, then shifts to the value and importance of parental management of children, which is a major focus of her concern.

During this section of the session, Lankton suggests that she may in fact have those skills to be parental with her son, but inhibits their expression as a function of her self-criticism. Before proceeding to another, more complicated idea, Lankton secures agreement from Joan about the pre-ceding suggestion or frame. Thus, throughout the session, he establishes a positive response set that creates an important foundation for the next piece of work.

An important notion in Ericksonian work is the idea of the continuing development of rapport between the client and therapist and the strategic use of self by the therapist. Thus, in the early part of the session, Joan describes her visits with her son, and her anxiety about the mother–son relationship. As a part of this anxiety, she anticipates her son's eventual departure and her "falling apart." Lankton listens and tells of his experi-ence with the comings and goings of his own adult son and of himself in relation to his (Lankton's) father. At this point, he gently suggests that "falling apart" seems less descriptive for him than feeling sad. This is a simple reframing of the client's idea while simultaneously legitimizing and positively connoting her feelings.

Lankton then asks Joan about a previous hypnotic experience. He mentions that he often uses hypnosis in his work with clients, and that it might be a useful tool to use in managing anxiety. Lankton further sug-gests that people, when experiencing hypnosis, attend to what is relevant and ignore what is not. He states that "talking about your son coming up in a month is very relevant, I'm sure, and if not now, will be soon." Lankton (1) introduces the idea and utility of hypnosis, (2) suggests that she will make the appropriate meanings based on her needs, and (3) that if she does not now, then she will soon. This is a nice example of seeding or offering ideas now that will be developed in the future.

Lankton asks Joan when she thinks her anxiety began. Here she shares her history of her mother's death when Joan was only three. In anticipation of his hypnotic intervention, Lankton asks how she dealt with the loss of her mother and how she comforted herself. Joan indicates that she did not receive much comfort from others, and that her father, who was alcoholic, never talked about her mother or was able to provide much in the way of emotional support. When Joan states that she cannot picture her mother, Lankton, in a very personal response, shares that he recently lost his own mother, and that he has trouble picturing her. He says, in normalizing her experience, "You don't know that that's probably a common thing. . . ." Erickson believed that nothing can happen in therapy in the absence of the therapeutic relationship. Lankton is quite genuine in sharing himself, a fact that is not lost upon Joan and the therapeutic relationship.

Lankton then shifts from the past to the present, and asks Joan about her relationship with her son. Joan suggests that because of physical dis-tance and time apart, her son probably does not value her as a mother. In the subsequent interaction, Lankton directly challenges Joan's assump-tions, and directly suggests that now may be the time for a discussion about Joan and her ex-husband's divorce. Following the discussion of her family history, this proposed discussion is a clear suggestion for Joan to communicate with her son in a way that she would have wanted her father to communicate with her. Lankton then specifically suggests a long scenario of how such a discussion might unfold. Within this scenario, Lankton suggests a useful way to communicate in contrast to a less useful manner with an anecdote about Julio Iglesias. He then shows how such a conversation might proceed. In this conversation, he predicts what negative thoughts Joan might have and offers alternative responses. In a somewhat paradoxical manner, Lankton indirectly suggests that she directly say to herself in the conversation with her son, "I love him. That's all there is to it. I love him, and that's what I want to talk about today. I want to enhance him as a person." Continuing, he suggests coming back in a few days to offer her son a further opportunity for discussion, while suggesting that internally he may be open to his mother, while externally he acts like a typical noncommunicative teenager. Suggesting developmental change over time, Lankton tells an anecdote of how one father, who felt distant from his son, but continued to be the best parent he could be, learned after his son had grown up that the son had respected and appreciated him all along. This anecdote parallels Joan's current experience with her own son, and thus implies a possible positive change in the future.

In the next part of the session, Lankton shifts the focus to Joan's connection to others, particularly men. Here he listens carefully to her presentation and is sensitive to her feelings. He then reflects back to her his understanding of her experience, which she confirms. During this series of exchanges, Lankton goes into to a fair amount of detail about what her internal dialogue might be, while suggesting a more positive and adaptive dialogue. For example, he says, "Rather than saying I'm weak because I'm feeling nervous and anxious and a void, you could very well be thinking that the world needs not to disenfranchise people because they are not married, childbearing consumers"—to which Joan agrees. A key aspect of this interaction is a very effective attempt at depathologizing Joan's view of her own behavior. Lankton captures the essence of her feelings, which she acknowledges, and then suggests that such feelings and behaviors are normal, useful, and adaptive at this time. Lankton underscores the Ericksonian belief that people make the best choices they can given their current limitations, which also implies that different times may call for different behaviors.

When Joan suggests that perhaps she should have a nervous breakdown and just get it over with, Lankton challenges her directly, and with humor asks how she came to have such an idea. This line of questioning is similar to Michael White's externalizing the problem. Lankton, by asking questions in this manner, is indirectly suggesting that whatever her concern is, it is not her, but something that is separate from her. Again, this seems to be an effective attempt at depathologizing her self-perceptions and suggesting a normalizing framework. Lankton offers a shift from the idea of having a nervous breakdown to taking a break, to which Joan agrees. This is a nice example of utilizing what the client offers initially and shifting to perhaps a more adaptive possibility.

## Transition to Hypnosis

At this point in the session, Lankton is shifting to helping Joan to access the desired resources she needs in interactions with her son and others. He begins this process by asking her when she last "practiced feeling proud and happy." She responds by laughing and saying that she cannot re-member. Lankton jokingly asks how she can expect to be an expert and not have practiced what to do. Lankton and Joan share a story of how they both had lost pictures of their children and the importance of replacing them. At this point, Lankton asks Joan to close her eyes and picture a series of photographs of her son, and to show him (Lankton) how she experi-ences that feeling of pride that she said she never practiced. Lankton then suggests to her a range of different feelings (laughter, tenderness, etc.) in viewing the pictures of her son.

Here Lankton moves to the essence of the clinical work when he sug-gests, by way of an apposition of opposites, that Joan shift from picturing her son's growing up to seeing herself become smaller and smaller, to being a child of three or four. Lankton seeks to establish the positive feelings that Joan has as a mother to her son, and then suggests she "skip back along the series of pictures of yourself as an increasingly younger girl, but hold onto those same feelings. . . . you've had as you make a picture of yourself as younger and younger. So you can picture that feeling of yourself even as three-year-old Joan with a feeling of a caring mother in your heart."

## Back to the Future

With this scenario established, Lankton provides very clear instruc-tions for Joan as the child to experience the feelings of a caring mother in her heart. Using conscious/unconscious dissociation, Lankton asks her conscious mind to be "aware of your being a loving mother while your unconscious is holding onto a sense that you're imaging that three- or four-year-old inside." Lankton then gives Joan very specific instructions as to what she might say from the future to the three-year-old self of the past. He suggests that Joan make a deal with the child, which is, "You be the mother to her who's proud and amazed and sad and tender and happy and loving and caring if she can be the little girl for you to provide the continuity that you need on the side of that equation." This, for me, is the heart and soul of this therapeutic session, to provide an opportunity for Joan to re-create and/or revise her childhood experiences based on her ability to be a mother to her son. Her ability to be a self-confident mother now will be enhanced as a function of her remothering of herself as a child. This is the therapeutic equivalent of Escher's hand drawing itself.

Lankton further suggests that when the child within needs the mother from the adult Joan "she will signal by way of a feeling in your heart or stomach that the child has a need." This suggestion is particularly useful because Lankton anticipates that Joan as a matter of course will have some anxious feelings in the future. As such, Lankton has reframed these feelings as (1) a signal from the child within that (2) can be responded to and managed by the capable adult mother figure. This is a clear example of utilizing that which the client presents. During this process of reparenting, Lankton indirectly suggests a dissociative experience for Joan. He reminds Joan that she is sitting comfortably in his office while she can "watch the picture of the grown-up Joan watching the little Joan." At this point, Lankton offers a trance-deepening experience, and then directly suggests that Joan further comfort the sad child who lost her own mother, and he suggests that she say, "You're still going to grow up and be a wonderful person and a beautiful child, and I love you."

Lankton continues, in a vein similar to Erickson's in the "February man," to provide Joan with the opportunity to comfort and support Joan the child through various developmental stages, such as "riding the bicycle around the block" and "when you lived through that DPT shot." Lankton tells Joan, "Take all the time you need, because being a mother is a lifetime job and being a father is a lifetime job." This statement not only speaks to the process of Joan's parenting herself, but also indirectly comments on her relationship with her son.

Lankton proceeds to tell Joan a story about another client who was saved as a small boy from falling plaster over his bed by the appearance of a "ghost," seemingly there to warn him about this impending disaster. The boy's father indicated that ghost fit the description of the boy's long-deceased grandfather. Lankton distances himself from the ghost story when he quotes his client as wondering why he ever mentioned it because he (the client) did not believe in ghosts. Lankton, denying that he himself believes in ghosts, then offers to Joan the meaning of the ghost story and the work they (Lankton and Joan) have just completed when he suggests that perhaps the spirit of "your mother has been satisfied in realizing that you have hit upon a way that frees her now to rest in peace knowing that the little girl she abandoned can bring a smile to the face of her mother, who really needs to have a smile brought to her face by a child on a regular basis."

## Testing the Work

To test the effectiveness of their work, Lankton asks Joan to picture herself in the present beginning to feel anxious, and then to ask the little girl to help her remember what giggling sounds like "so that the little girl knows that she really is valuable to the grown-up, too." Lankton gives personal examples of how his own little daughter is valuable to him. He then suggests that Joan switch from watching the little girl interacting with the adult Joan to watching herself interact with her son in the near future, and he suggests that she feel proud that she is doing what is important for her son. He further suggests that she thank the little girl for her smile, because when she talks to a little boy who has been separated from his mother, she will be able to use that smile. After accessing the needed resources and building new associative learnings, Lankton can now state fairly directly how Joan will be able to use these learnings in the immediate future.

Emphasizing this theme, Lankton suggests that she practice her new learnings. He states that there is "no reason to have a beautiful boy if you can't have some of the good feelings of connection and joy." To solidify the work, Lankton tells her to take the next few minutes to think about the various ways in which she can "find avenues back to these ideas." Simultaneously, he suggests that she think ahead to the future and use self-hypnosis or dream (a suggestion of comparable alternatives) about using these new skills. He offers a range of direct and indirect suggestions covering everyday occurrences in which Joan can use her new learnings (i.e., holidays, birthdays, "no one called me back on the telephone" days, etc.).

After returning to the conscious state, Joan considerably misjudges how much time has elapsed, which Lankton utilizes to reinforce that her unconscious mind was doing important work. When she states that coming out of trance was slow, Lankton answers, "I guess that's your sign that there was some useful material that you want to practice." "Practice" is a key word, because its importance was mentioned so frequently in the hypnotic work. Joan readily agrees with Lankton's observation, thus reinforcing the value of practice.

When Joan, who was quite articulate about her negative feelings, seems less clear about describing her current feelings, Lankton seizes this opportunity to suggest her lack of experience in having, and therefore describing, positive feelings. Lankton then presents a series of anecdotes about looking up words in the dictionary. This entire discussion focuses on such words as noble, dignity, polite, and courteous, which, Lankton states, "is the warm regard for the dignity of others. Sounds good, doesn't it?" And Joan agrees.

## Conclusion

This case represents a very clear and well-executed example of one approach to Ericksonian therapy. Lankton hears Joan's story and seeks to emphasize her strengths. Prior to trance, he and she agree on what feelings and positive interactions she would like to have with her son. Lankton then utilizes what was missing from Joan's own past (a mother who died early in the client's life) to help Joan (1) reparent herself in the way her mother would have had she lived, and (2) then to use that parenting skill to be the mother she desires for her own son. Once this belief and this experience are established, Lankton directly suggests that she practice them in trance, and anticipates her using these resources in the context in which they are needed. In concluding the hypnotic work, a wide range of posthypnotic suggestions connected to everyday stimuli are given that, instead of provoking anxiety and negative feelings, can serve as a stimulus to access the desired feelings.

Finally, as the session started in the conscious state, discussing Joan's concerns, it concludes in the conscious state, emphasizing her strengths and the importance of practicing these new feelings, with which she is in clear agreement. Erickson believed that people make the best choices they can given their perceived limitations, and that the resources needed for change lie within. Lankton, in this case, underscores that point beautifully. He and Joan create the context for the development and use of existing resources to support an overarching change in her self-perception.

# Commentary on a Therapy with Joan

## Robert Schwarz, Psy.D.

I have been asked to comment on what made the therapy session under review so successful. The problem is that not only can we not know precisely what aspect of the therapy is responsible for the patient's improvement, but we also cannot know if the therapy is responsible at all for the improvement. What we can do is understand the process of the therapy in order to make inferences about what may have been therapeutic for this client. I might as well state from the outset that if this were a movie, I would give it five stars. My intention though is not simply to laud the therapist. Rather, it is to point out what was helpful in order to further the craft of Ericksonian therapy.

From a more scientific standpoint, it will be interesting to discover if there is any interrater reliability among the commentaries about what transpired. Or are these analyses merely projections of the writers' points of view. A different tactic would be to consider internal reliability. In other words, does the therapist do what he says he does? Fortunately, we have plenty of information about how Lankton says he does therapy.

Lankton (1985) has described a state-of-consciousness model of hypnosis. He quotes Tart (1975): "A State of Consciousness (SoC) is considered to be a 'unique, dynamic pattern or configuration of psychological structures, an active system of psychological subsystems'" (p. 5). An SoC can be thought of as an "SoC molecule" consisting of various "atomic substructures." These can include feeling states, patterns of attention, degree of sympathetic and parasympathetic arousal, quality of internal dialogue, and mental images, memories, and so on. During everyday life, we use different SoCs for adapting to our varied roles and situations.

Ericksonian therapy is based on the viewpoint that problems and psychiatric symptoms develop when clients become stuck in an SoC or pattern of SoCs that lacks the resources needed to meet the social and behavioral

Address correspondence to Robert Schwarz, Psy.D., IACT, P.O. Box 326, Villanova, PA 19085.

demands confronting them (Lankton, 1985). Erickson viewed trance as a particular psychological state that made it easier to reassociate and reorganize one's inner experience (Erickson & Rossi, 1979). Successful therapy involves the reassociation and reorganization of one's associations, memories, and experiences (in other words, SoCs and patterns of SoC activation) in such a manner that the client has the requisite resources to solve the demands that life has placed on him or her (Lankton, 1985).

Additionally, SoCs are organized and maintained at different logical levels. These include unconscious patterns of experience, conscious beliefs, interpersonal communication, social roles, and family organization (Lankton, 1985; Lankton & Lankton, 1986). For therapy to be effective, interventions (especially brief interventions) must be aimed at whatever combination of levels is necessary to reorganize the client's SoCs and provide sufficient reinforcement to maintain the new organization. Of course, it is even better to make interventions at all levels that interdependently reinforce the therapeutic outcome. In the therapy under review, Lankton does intervene on all of the logical levels described, which may also account for the therapeutic outcome.

We can understand the session as the deconstruction of specific dysfunctional SoCs and the construction of more functional SoCs. The first segment of the therapy is clearly more conversational and interactional. There is an obvious cocreation of an ongoing sequence of events. The client and the therapist shape each other's response. Since this is a therapeutic interaction, the client is inviting the therapist to work on certain goals. The therapist is responding to the client in some manner, and inviting the client to consider certain ideas and points of view, as well as certain other goals. There is a negotiation process happening. While it is important to meet the client at his or her model of the world and utilize what the client brings to therapy (Lankton & Lankton, 1983), the therapist cannot stay in the client's model of the world, because that model is what keeps the client stuck. The therapist needs to organize his or her own thinking and behavior in a manner that is inconsistent with the client's limited model of the world and is consistent with a more functional model that is negotiated between client and therapist. In the case under consideration, this is done in the first half of the therapy session.

One final consideration regarding SoCs merits attention, namely the SoC of the therapist while doing therapy. Obviously, the SoC of a practitioner of an Ericksonian approach to therapy differs from that of a biological psychiatrist. Furthermore, even among Ericksonians there are significant differences in SoCs. From Lankton's writings, as well as my contact with him, I will suggest certain aspects of the operation of his SoC. Lankton is looking for strengths and resources to build upon. For instance, early in the session, the client starts to talk about the only time she feels self-confident. Lankton responds, "You have legitimate power." This comment punctuates and emphasizes this strength and resource.

Lankton will also look for dysfunctional aspects of the client's SoC that are communicated interpersonally. He will make sure not to reinforce these, and, in fact, to disrupt them. This type of communication is the interpersonal equivalent of the second step of hypnotic induction, depotentiating habitual frameworks and belief systems (Erickson & Rossi, 1979). In this case, there are repeated interventions to avoid support for and to undermine the client's self-criticism, as well as her stance of passivity.

The ensuing disruption then leads to the interpersonal equivalent of the third step of induction, unconscious search (Erickson & Rossi, 1979). This happens not just for the client, but also for the therapist. By preventing an organization of the interview around the client's usual way of thinking, Lankton will try to ascertain the client's underlying presuppositions upon which much of her dysfunctional SoC is built. Since the client is not allowed to organize around her usual way of thinking, deeper presuppositions are more likely to come to the surface. Since the therapist is open to, and searching for, deeper presuppositions, he is likely to notice them. Once one is detected, Lankton will challenge and reframe it. If the client allows his or her presupposition to change, then therapeutic change must necessarily occur.

It is this process that leads to the phenomenon of what I have called the "Lankton spin." The Lankton spin is the unusual angle from which he usually delivers the therapy. Witnesses, and presumably the client, have the experience of "I never thought of it that way." This phenomenon is a result of the detection and the challenge of an underlying presupposition. In the case with Joan, this happens when Lankton raises the issue that Joan does not practice feeling proud and happy. As we will see later, this theme becomes the keystone for the hypnotic therapy.

Finally, once hypnosis is under way, Lankton takes great care to interweave suggestions so that they are mutually reinforcing at a variety of logical levels, and so that the "elicited experiences are arranged into a network of associations that help clients form a new map of conduct" (Lankton, 1985, p. 38). He also makes sure that the work is associated to the client's future social context (Lankton & Lankton, 1983) in a variety of manners.

## Part 1. The Therapeutic Interview

There are several themes to the interventions in the first segment. Each theme will be presented with several examples from the transcript. The first theme addresses Joan's self-effacement and self-criticism. The interventions include interrupting her actual self-critical dialogue during the session, and normalizing her mistakes and difficulties so that it is hard to feel self-critical about them. These interventions start immediately.

C: I know. Her checklist was a little tough. It was almost like I could check off everything, and then yet again...I...you know...

L: Oh, you're like me when you...if it takes hours to fill those things out.

They are followed immediately by this interchange:

C: And she'd say, "Now, don't take a long time. Just, you know, go through it."

L: I don't know...did I...are you...are you employed and taking off work to come here now?[1]

He then addresses these issues consciously. And we see how the client begins to move out of the self-critical place, and then how Lankton marks this out.

L: In that your score that when you criticized yourself may be different and may have kept you from checking such thing as "able to give orders," checked that particular one, thinking, "Well, I don't know," and you leave it blank. So that self-criticism may have been operating when you filled it out and could have kept that score lower.

C: Probably. I 'm pretty hard on myself. I mean...I...in my job I have to have a certain amount of control over a situation and I do...

L: Yeah.

C: The only time that I really feel that I'm in control or that I have any self-confidence is when I'm at work.

L: Uh-huh. Oh. Uh-huh.

C: The only time I'm...behind a desk and there doing my job and it's the only time that I feel that...

L: You have legitimate power.

There is a second theme that communicates "we do our experience," it does not just happen. In other words, this intervention challenges the existential stance of passivity that so often undermines therapy. This is demonstrated in the following transactions.

C: I mean my feelings overpower it, so I feel a bit insecure, you know, because I'm going to have to say good-bye to him. Then I tend to fall apart, I'm already preparing, you know, not to deal with it very well.

L: Does that work out? Do you succeed 100 percent of the time? Do you then fall apart?

C: Yeah, well, the last two times I've been pretty good at, you know, keeping it together, which, you know, is kind of a breakthrough for me.

L: When does he come again?

C: He'll be here the end of June [in four weeks].

L: Are you already preparing to fall apart or do you wait...is there still, like a Labor Day weekend...or how do you do that? When do you know when to start? Do you need like a special amount of shopping time ahead to know...?

C: No, I just...

L: Only so many shopping days to get my falling apart together?

The third theme is a bit more complex. Lankton communicates the following group of ideas: Joan is not as sick as she thinks she is. She has been facing difficult challenges. She has not been using the most appropriate tools in her toolbox to solve these problems. These interventions challenge her perception of herself on the level of belief and social role. The specific types of interventions that are used include the following.

*Implication and Presupposition*

L: So, if the world somehow suddenly or accurately demands that you be...demonstrating dominant behaviors, then it would stand to reason that you'd get a little bit nervous because you *don't think you have those in your toolbox.* [Italics added]

L: There's a lot of easy outs you could take that you've not taken. And perhaps you took easy outs in the past, and you're remembering things that were easy outs that you took, but you sound very willing to be a fighter.

When asked whether she can visualize her mother, Joan describes how she is unable to do so. The therapist responds: "I can't, by the way, particularly picture my mother, and she died fairly recently. You don't know that that's probably a common thing, even if you had seen her for 10 more or 20 more years."

*Reframing*

In response to Joan's talking about how she "falls apart" when it comes time for her son to leave after a visit, Lankton states, "But I wouldn't ask myself...I wouldn't say it's falling apart, you know. I mean, that's the word that really struck oddly with me. I would think it might be maybe 'sad'..."

Later, in response to Joan's description of how overwhelmed, insecure, and anxious she feels, and that she needs Xanax, the following reframings are used.

L: You know, you talk like a person who is expressing a real American, I guess, or maybe it's a world-wide problem that leads a lot of people to get married for no good reason other than to avoid this fear, and to have kids for no reason other than to avoid that emptiness, and to get involved with drugs or something for no good reason other than for that sense of...

C: I've done it all—gotten married and got involved in drugs.

L: And who, given nothing to do, especially because of some other little problem, doesn't mean they're not employable because of their education or their race or something like that, or their sex, whatever has kept them from overcoming their geography or something has kept them from being employable, then they're a prime target to become victim of a mental health hierarchy that is all too willing to give them a label, give them drugs, and the more you participate in it, the more you feel more what you wanted to avoid, sort of, because it...and...So, in a way, you're grappling with really the "human condition," you know. And I don't know anyone who has particularly said, "Grappling with the human condition is a lovely piece of cake."

*Gentle Challenges*

Here humor and exaggeration are used to challenge Joan's presuppositions. It is interesting to notice that her basic premise is accepted and then utilized by turning it back on itself. This can be a very effective pattern. So if she is waiting for a breakdown (like waiting for a bus), then "now" is a good time. The bus has arrived.

C: Sometimes I think I'm waiting for this...I'm waiting to have the nervous breakdown I should have had when my son was given to his father. You know, I never...

L: Well, now's a good time. I've got 45 minutes. Perhaps...

C: I never [laughing]...it's true that I...that's when I say, you know, I...Sometimes I feel like I'm ready...I'm at that point, you know, when I get into a depressed point. But I don't allow that to happen. And I never have allowed that to happen from the time that he was...

L: Well, you're off work now. You know that commercial that says you haven't got time for the pain? Well, you've got time. Go ahead and have it.

C: You know, I could have gone into a hospital, and then I thought, no, that would look worse on my records, you know, back then when he was taken away from me so that I fought, you know, and...

L: Why do you think you have to have a nervous breakdown?

C: No, I mean sometimes when I...

L: To be complete? It's sort of like, you know...

C: No, it's like, let me get it over with, and then I'll be fine for the rest of my life.

L: Yeah, right. Where did you get this idea that there's a nervous break-down in the box that has to be? It doesn't say that in the instruction manual. Okay, lose child, go home, have a nervous breakdown, pick up parts, put them in the box.

C: Well, I think, you know, I'm "recovering" too from drugs and alcohol, and I have had a couple setbacks in the past year and a half.

L: But you need to answer that question. Where did you get the idea... that's the predominant thing that keeps coming around. Why does it? Where do you get the impression that that's part of the deal?

C: I, you know, I don't know. I think it's just...you're right. It's just in my head where I feel like I just want to take a break from feeling everything.

L: That's cool to take a break, but having a nervous breakdown isn't an especially good break...Bimini is a much better idea. Bahamas is good.

C: Right. Well, then, I can deal with that. I can deal with that. No, I mean, there are times when I'm tired. You know, where I just want to shut everything off, but I know that I can't do that. You know, I can't. You know, I have to function, I have to be there. You know, I can't...I used to escape and get high and stoned and, you know, not care, and then realize the next morning that those things are there and are still going to be there. You know...am I making any sense?

L: You're making a lot of sense, except that you skip past the part where you don't have an explanation and you think you've answered that for yourself. But you didn't. And it seems like you should, really.

C: Answer myself about why I deserve a nervous breakdown?

L: Well, yeah. Why do you think it has to be that?

C: I mean, it's not that I think it has to, but sometimes I feel...Like Mother's Day. Mother's Day was really rough on me and I felt... sometimes I feel like I'm fighting it.

It is important to notice that he keeps challenging her. This is hypnosis. It is the same structure of suggesting that the pinkie will lift, followed by a tentative response on the part of the subject, followed by more sugges-tions by the hypnotist. The questioning and the confusion keep Joan on an unconscious search for her own inner meaning. This leads to the turning point in the therapy, the issue of feeling pride as a mother. This will be discussed shortly.

The fourth theme revolves around the framing and introduction of the tools that Joan needs to use to solve problems. The discussion and stories here act as seeding (Zeig, 1985) for the main interventions that will follow during the hypnosis. The tools include the following.

*The Ability to Be in a One-Up Position and Not Worry*
*About What the Child Thinks*

L: You could just bring it up. You say, "Have you ever wanted to talk about why we got divorced, why you went with your father, or anything like that?" "I don't know"; that's the proper answer for his age. "Well, in that case, I think yes. We're going to talk about it," you say. And then you say, "Let me tell you a few things that are on my mind." And he probably won't participate much. He'll probably just take it in and think about it.

*Recognition of the Importance of Nonverbal Communicating When Dealing*
*with Children, so That They Will Be Influenced in a Positive Manner*

L: Let's think about how to terminate it just for a minute. Because if you terminate it by a look on your face that says, "Oh, God. I didn't think that could be worth going into," that's more information that he's taking in. Kids especially, and in the unconscious part of all of us, as well, are really good at making sense of what just occurred onstage by what occurs as an offstage line. So, if, you know, you heard Julio Iglesias sing a wonderful bunch of numbers, or something, on a stage in Las Vegas, and then they forgot to turn his mike off and he walked offstage and said, "Now, I've got those damn people out...that damn job over with...and those stupid people out of there," that would just ruin the whole performance. So, and if you heard the mike on and he said, "What a lovely audience," and "They made me feel so warm," and you'd think, "Gee, he really was a cool guy." So that offstage line helps you understand. So, likewise, when this whole thing is over and you say, "Any questions," and he says, "No," and you say, "Well, if you have any questions, you be sure to ask them, okay, sweetheart?" And he goes, "Okay." Then you don't want to go, "Oh, Christ, I knew it wasn't going to do any good." You want to take what kind of dignity you want to portray to him. You don't want to show him, "Gee, I'm afraid he doesn't love me." You don't want to show him...you do want to show him, "I love him. That's all there is to it." "I love him," and that's what I want to talk about today. "I want to enhance him as a person." The "someday when he grows up, he's going to be a better man because we had this talk, even if he doesn't say so now" look on your face. That's the offstage-line incident. Then you look at him and he goes "Okay," then just kind of glaring through him to see the man that he's going to become some day and be happy with his inner happinesses.

Underneath a very interesting story and series of suggestions about how to communicate congruently, there is a tremendous presupposition. *She is a mother who can enhance her son.*

### The Ability to Think About Outcomes of Actions in the Distant Future

This ability (as opposed to thinking about the immediate future) is suggested through a metaphor about a man who lost his son in a custody battle, but after many years, the son came to realize that the father was okay.

### The Importance of Feeling Pride

C: But it's so negative. Mother's Day. Mother's Day should be a positive day for me. I mean, I'm the mother of a beautiful son, and I was depressed Mother's Day. I was, you know . . . and I fight with myself, saying, you know, try . . . why . . .

L: And you practice so very much feeling proud and happy. I'll just bet. When was the last time that you practiced feeling proud and happy?

C: I can't remember [laughing].

L: Well then, how in the hell do you expect to be an expert as the clock turns midnight and not even do what you practiced? I have a brother-in-law who's an expert classical guitarist, and at midnight he could play classical guitar when the clock turned to "Classical Guitarist Day," . . . But he practices all the time at that. So, I was thinking you probably must have practiced being proud and happy if you thought you were just going to "kick it in" at midnight. You don't practice that? Oh, God, you're as bad as my seven-year-old.

C: In fact, I go up to people begging them to ask me about my son so I can brag about him, you know, and that doesn't happen too often.

As stated earlier, this is the fulcrum point of the therapy. We now have a goal that is positive and future looking. It is the existence of something rather than the lack of something else. It has ramifications at all levels of experience. It is relevant both to the here and now and to future experiences with Joan's son, as well as Joan's past relationship with her mother. These issues will be addressed in the hypnosis.

Here is one further refinement that is relevant to understanding how this therapy was so successful. When Lankton asks Joan to show him pictures, she does not have any. At first he responds, "Good practicing! I am convinced now." She then gives an explanation of how she lost her pictures. Lankton's first comment is at risk of being felt as critical and shaming. He appears to catch himself and changes tactics. He normalizes and depathologizes her "failure" by telling how he also lost his wallet full of pictures. These types of interventions, as well as the mistake and recovery, demonstrate the importance of having an assessment and diagnosis that are functionally useful. If the diagnosis is that the client is overly self-critical, then the therapist knows to avoid engaging in interactions that follow that pattern. In some other therapy, one might be tempted to follow the pathological path. The therapist might explore in greater detail how the client does not allow herself to feel pride. This would only lead to increasing her shame, the exact opposite of the therapeutic goal. The hypothesis was stated. It appeared to have been accepted by the client. The loss of pictures is a behavioral example of how she fails to "practice" (a state, not a trait). So, there is no reason to rub her face in it. Rather, just get on with teaching her how to feel pride, which is exactly what is done next. This then segues almost seamlessly into the more formal aspect of the hypnosis.

## Part 2. Formal Hypnosis

The first half of the formal trance is spent on the issue of a parent feeling pride for her child. We cannot go into every detail of the transcript, but we can note some important patterns that probably contributed to a successful outcome. At first, Lankton meets Joan in her own context, namely, her son. She is then asked to access feelings of pride about him. Once a bit of pride has been retrieved, it is built upon and strengthened. She is asked to experience it across multiple modalities: visual, kinesthetic, self-talk. By representing it across multiple modalities, the response becomes stronger and more difficult to extinguish (Bandura, 1969).

L: Pick up any feeling of pride or happiness that you have on seeing his beautiful development. Because that's what those pictures are for, aren't they? They're sort of like anchors to having located, "Oh God, he's cool," and pick up a good feeling. . . and a fantasy has some . . . and pick up a good feeling. Of course, good feelings might have some smile attached. Some good feelings might have some sort of, like, laughter attached. Some good feelings might have tenderness attached. So they're all of the same theme, but the whole group is really your pride in being the mother.

Consider the very next suggestion:

*L:* When you scan that, can you feel a feeling of change as you do? That's
practicing! It's working!

Not only does this ratify the previous suggestions, but it ties the entire
presuppositional shift of practicing pride to the hypnotherapy.

The trance is deepened and the feelings of pride are stabilized, and Joan
is given a self-anchor or cue to be able to hold onto the feeling of being a
mother who has pride. The next segment of the therapy revolves around
dissociative review and redecision work (Lankton & Lankton, 1983), with
the older, resourceful Joan being the mother to the younger Joan. There are
several nuances that are important to note. First, the feelings of pride that
older Joan will use have been retrieved and strengthened *before* the redecision work is done. Many times, therapists just tell clients to nurture
and love their inner child. The problem is that they have not accessed the
necessary representation of a nurturing, loving parent.

Second, the redecision work is framed as bilateral. There is a deal
between the parts. The inner child gets to feel the pride and love and protection of a loving mother. The older Joan gets to feel the feelings of the joy
and sadness of a little girl. She also gets to know that she is valued and
needed by that part.

Consider the following suggestion.

*L:* First of all, ask her to know that... to give you that head nod again, if
she [the little girl] realizes that you feel like a proud mother toward her
and a loving mother toward her.

In context, this just looks like part of an ongoing dialogue between the
parts. However, there is an incredible implication in this sentence. If the
little girl answers in the affirmative, then Joan has inner confirmation that
tells her that she is a proud and loving mother. It is an analogue to the
perspective of "someone else." So that if Joan is having a bad day in real
time, there can be that inner voice that says, "They may not know you are
a good and loving mother, but *I know* you are." These are the very things
she needs to be able to maintain in the face of the real difficulties in the
outside world.

The following series of suggestions contain several important aspects.
First, there is an acceptance and a utilization of female-gender–based needs
for self-esteem coming through relationship, rather than the male orientation of being a separate individual. Second, the principle of interlocking
the suggestions on a variety of logical levels is apparent. The use of
giggling as an unconscious pattern of experience and an interpersonal
communication is tied to beliefs and social roles of being proud and of
helping out a parent. The entire complex of associations is then suggested
to be a replacement for anxiety.[2]

L: I think you should go ahead and tell that there's another part of the secret, which is that you'd be a lot happier too if you knew somebody continually needed you and was happy that you were happy to be needed. And the two of you could exchange that happiness with each other. And have each other to be around for one another. And, if that's the case, then maybe you can even hear her giggle. That'd be pretty nice to hear her giggle again. I know that when my little girl giggles, it's about the happiest sound I've ever heard. My little boy giggles okay, but my little girl giggles so much better. And let the sound of that little girl that you love, and once were and still are, just echo and vibrate throughout your bones. Let the giggle replace the vibration of anxiety, in fact. Ask her if it would be okay with her if you used her giggle to replace that sense of anxiety. If she wouldn't feel too put upon if you use it in that way because you sure could use it. I asked my little girl once when I was going on a trip if it would be okay, whenever I started to feel sad and lonely, if I remembered her giggle and helped the giggle to come instead of the tears, and she said, "It would make me as proud as the day I got my DPT shot, Daddy."

The next segment of the therapy changes the perceptual position from which Joan understands her past and her self. Instead of seeing herself as the child who was deprived of her mother (ergo, there is something wrong with the child), there is a lengthy intervention about how it was her mother who missed out on the opportunity to have joy and pride in watching the child grow up.[3] In the context of Joan's therapy, this not a cute or a clever reframe. Joan understands quite well how much she is missing by not being with her son. The odds are that Joan has never thought about her mother's experience (and her relationship with Joan) from the knowledge base of a mother who cannot be with her child. Therefore, there is the potential for a deep shift in her presuppositional framework.

The point of view of her mother is further elaborated by the ghost story. Once again, there is a utilization of what Joan likely feels with regard to her son (she hopes he will be okay without her). Not only does this story play upon the wish to know that our parents will love us and protect us, even from beyond the grave, it also suggests that even after many years, and even after skipping a generation, one can repair the injuries to loved ones that one committed. Furthermore, it is suggested that:

L: Maybe, in some way, that spirit of your mother has been satisfied in realizing you hit upon a way that frees her now to rest in peace knowing that the little girl that she abandoned can bring a smile to the face of her mother, who really needs a smile brought to her face by a child on a regular basis; whose needs to find a child have found one who needs a mother. And they both agree to it and spend a great deal of time beginning the process of mothering, daughtering, sharing, needing, nurturing, and giggling.

If we accept the idea that we repeat scripts based upon internal patterns that we carry in our unconscious (Berne, 1972), then it logically follows that if the pattern is changed, the script will change. Since Joan's mother can now finally feel free and relieved, then the pattern for Joan is that she also can be free and relieved.

The remainder of the session is dedicated to the goals of solidifying and further intertwining the previous work that will help make it an indivisible gestalt, as well as of linking the internal work to a client's social context (Lankton & Lankton, 1983). One particularly nice moment where both goals are accomplished simultaneously is the reframing of giggling as a nice way to fall apart *with people*, followed by an affect protocol for safety, followed by suggestions that shape attitude with respect to children receiving benefit by knowing that they were able to bring joy to an adult, followed by posthypnotic suggestions regarding remembering nonverbal facial expressions that communicate value to the child.

Joan is then asked to let the new experience from the intrapsychic interactions between the inner child and the adult be useful in Joan's interactions with her son. She is asked to practice a discussion with her son (alluding to the very beginning of the therapy). Then she is asked to include in the rehearsal, feeling pride. Finally, there are a series of specific and generative posthypnotic suggestions that hearken back to earlier in the session, as well as link the work to Joan's future and social context:

L: And I just know that having the tools placed in your hand, you'll use them. So take your time for the next couple of minutes to think about the various ways in which you can find avenues back to these ideas. And simultaneously think ahead to times when you'll be sleeping at night and dreaming, or awake purposely, and sit down and meditate, if you want to, and use self-hypnosis, or you can just dream about them, night dreams or daydreams. Or when you're alone, and want, just think about it in some way again. Reinstall, replace, wipe out any feelings of unpleasantness that you're having. Think about the times you're going to want to use these feelings, and let your unconscious find various avenues to bring them to mind in the future; or let your unconscious think ahead to when you're going to want to use these conscious memories, these experiences, in the future, to vividly learn, at the very first sign of dread and anxiety, detachment in living, in the next few weeks and all the years to come — and the holidays, the birthdays, the Mother's Days, the New Year's Days, the After Johnny Carson's Over

Days, the "no one called me back on the telephone again" days. And look forward to any improvements you can make through repeated practice.

## Summary

In 1983, Lankton and Lankton wrote about multiple embedded metaphors (MEMs). Some have chided the Lanktons about just going around and telling stories to clients, or teaching therapists how to tell MEMs as a cookie-cutter approach. Of course, this was never their intention. In this therapy, we can still see the general patterns of the MEM framework, even though metaphor was not used as formally as described in their 1983 book. Resources were retrieved and associated intrapsychically, affects and attitudes were shaped, and finally, the work was linked to the client's social context. The concept of "embedding" can now be seen as interlocking and recursive suggestions that mutually reinforce and stabilize SoCs on multiple logical levels. This allows clients to have well-represented SoCs and multiple pathways between those SoCs so they have flexibility in solving problems.

To briefly review, Lankton worked on at least the following logical levels:

1. Joan's verbal and nonverbal communication with her son.
2. Joan's tendency to criticize herself.
3. Joan's beliefs and social roles about herself with respect to falling apart, being a psychiatric patient and a poor mother.
4. Joan's social roles and family organization with respect to her own mother, as well as her son.
5. Joan's unconscious patterns of experience with respect to the relationship with her "inner child" and the resulting feelings of anxiety or giggling, shame versus pride, and isolation versus connection.

If we look at the theme of pride alone, at minimum it has been discussed in terms of Joan and her son, Joan toward little Joan, little Joan toward Joan, Joan in relation to her mother, and Joan's mother in relation to Joan. This type of elaboration on a concept that is full of "spin" and novelty is, at the very least, going to be intriguing and receiving of a great deal of processing time. It teaches Joan how to feel pride, rather than repeatedly telling her, "You are going to feel pride . . . you are going to feel pride . . ."

Assuming that it was the craft of the therapy that was responsible for the client's improvement, the clinical lessons to take from this work include:
1. Finding and perturbing a client's presuppositions.
2. Addressing the problem from multiple logical levels.

3. Taking care to weave suggestions so that they are interlocking and mutually reinforcing.

With respect to the question of internal reliability raised at the outset of this article, it is my opinion that the therapy is highly consistent with what Lankton says he does. One could now generate several hypotheses regarding the validity of the work. These would include testing each of the three clinical lessons just mentioned.

## Notes

1. This is as good a place as any to note an important pattern in the therapy. A suggestion for arm levitation is usually not a solitary suggestion. It is started, and then built upon. The implication of Lankton's interventions are meta-communications that say: "We are going to have an interpersonal relationship that is without self-criticism." When the subject does not have a big response, the therapist continues to disallow (meta-communicate) the self-criticism. The reader should note that the pattern of this communication is structurally and thematically identical to one of the content areas of the therapy, namely, a parent keeps telling a child over and over what the child needs to hear, even if the child does not acknowledge this in the here and now.
2. This style of interlocking suggestions happens throughout the therapy. It is well worth the reader's time to study them. In addition, due to the poor quality of the videotape, it was impossible to detect the client's minimal responses to suggestions. It is likely, however, that Lankton was including and ratifying responses as part of the suggestions.
3. Another Lankton spin.

## References

Bandura, A. (1969). *Principles of behavior modification*. New York: Holt Rinehart & Winston

Berne, E. (1972). *What do you say after you say hello?* New York: Grove.

Erickson, M., & Rossi, E. (1979). *Hypnotherapy, an exploratory casebook*. New York: Irvington.

Lankton, S. (1985). A states of consciousness model of Ericksonian hypnosis. In S. Lankton (Ed.), *Ericksonian Monographs*, Vol 1 (pp. 26–40).

Lankton, S., & Lankton, C. (1983). *The answer within*. New York: Brunner/Mazel.

Lankton, S., & Lankton, C. (1986). *Enchantment and intervention in the family: A framework of Ericksonian family therapy*. New York: Brunner/Mazel.

Tart, C. T. (1975). *States of consciousness*. New York: Dutton.

Zeig, J. (1985). *Experiencing Erickson: An introduction to the man and his work*. New York: Brunner/Mazel.

# Case Commentary: A Woman with Chronic Anxiety and Panic Attacks

## Richard Fisch, M.D.

It is a pleasure to be asked to review and comment on this fascinating interview. I have prided myself on doing therapy briefly, but it is extremely rare for me to help a patient resolve a problem in one session. (I usually need at least two.) It was with special interest, then, that I looked at what Stephen Lankton did, and my curiosity was all the greater since the presenting problem was of a chronic nature.

In principle, I really do not see any more difficulty in resolving a chronic problem than an acute one, since, for me, chronicity simply means that the patient has been doing the same thing, only longer. However, I know that it's hard to dispel the traditional pessimistic expectations about chronicity, since they usually operate on the implicit rather than the explicit level. Obviously, Lankton is not intimidated by chronicity.

Before I give my own explanation of why—or how—this case succeeded, some word of how I look at problems and therapy is needed; otherwise, the reader is likely to assume that I missed the significance of various events in the interview, that I overlooked "what is obviously there." One's frame of reference cannot but help define what is regarded as important, and, conversely, what is not significant. For example, a psychoanalytically oriented therapist not only would have a different explanation for success in this case than, say, a behaviorist, but even would not be likely to regard this case as successful. In the psychoanalytic frame of reference (model), symptom change, certainly durable change, can only come about by the patient's "working through" those "unconscious" processes that form the infrastructure of the presenting complaint. I do not mean to imply that such a model is less true than any others, but only that it is different, as is each therapist's frame of reference.

Address correspondence to Richard Fisch, M.D., 555 Middlefield Rd., Palo Alto, CA 94301.

As for the model I use, the basic assumptions are quite few:

1. Rather than viewing problems as some deviance from "normality," I think of them, simply, as complaints.
2. With little exception, I define complaints in behavioral or tangible terms; that is, who is doing (or saying) what and to whom is that a problem?
3. Rather than attach importance to the origin of a complaint, I see the problem as one of maintaining complained-about behavior, very much in the sense of "being stuck."
4. In order for a problem to be maintained, albeit unwittingly, it requires continuing effort.
5. Finally, and most central, the effort required to maintain a problem is, ironically, the persistence of a tack the complainant is expending in his or her intention to resolve or relieve the problem.

In general, then, the tasks of therapy are to aid in the relief of the complaint and to get the complainant to desist from his or her customary efforts at dealing with the problem (the "attempted solution"). In order to get the complainant to do that, it is usually necessary to have the client do something else, most often an action that is a negation of the attempted solution.

As for Lankton's case, it seems, from his introduction, that he had some background information and the results of some kind of self-assessment checklist that had been given to the client. The background information mentions diffuse and chronic complaints of "anxiety, hopelessness, and despair." It also describes a rather unhappy period in Joan's life when her husband and she divorced and she lost custody of her child (now 10 years old) because of her drug use and "promiscuous sexual behavior." Lankton starts the interview in a way that can be very useful; he immediately takes a one-down, nonauthoritarian position: "And I flew in and my ear hasn't cleared, so when you see me blowing this ear here..." This kind of position has the effect of helping the client to relax and so be more receptive to what the therapist says; at the same time, it informs the client that she has her work to do in the therapy since the therapist is not an all-powerful, all-knowing authority. (Erickson, for example, never tried to minimize the sequelae of his bouts with polio, and, instead, used them to obtain a nonverbal, one-down stance.) Lankton repeats his one-down position several times throughout the interview, partly by the revelation of difficulties or sad events that he has experienced in his own life: "When I get those phone calls when they want to sell me...." and "I can't... picture my mother, and she died fairly recently."

This kind of position can be very helpful to a client. It can prevent the barrier that is erected when the therapist takes a one-up stance (or is presumed to be doing so) and is perceived as having all the answers, judging the client for all her frailties, and being preachy. Since a therapist inherently is in a one-up position—the client is coming to the therapist's "turf," and is required to reveal his or her unsuccess in living to an expert who is presumed to be successful—it takes a little doing to offset that impression. I think that part of the success in this interview lies in Lankton's quickly setting up a stance of not being in a power position, of just being human.

After his brief introduction to the client, he spends some time with her going over the checklist. I don't see the benefit of doing that kind of thing, nor do I believe that it helps to explain the success of the interview. Rather, I think that checklists are counterproductive in therapy, implying that the client has some kind of unchangeable problem, a message of, "There's something wrong with you," versus "You're having trouble." Lankton does diminish the "harm" by dissociating himself from the checklist, pointing out that it was something arranged by his assistant, whose prior briefing "wasn't particularly enlightening." In any case, the checklist and the discussion of it did not interfere with the interview's success.

Throughout the session, Lankton takes the opportunity to make comments or ask questions in such a way that they set an implicit expectation of change or improvement. He does this in a number of ways, such as in engendering the idea that Joan has control over her emotions, that she is not a helpless victim of their vicissitudes:

C: Because I'm going to have to say goodbye to him. Then I tend to fall apart; I'm already preparing. . . not to deal with it very well.
L: Are you already preparing to fall apart or do you wait. . . or *how do you do that?* When do you *know* when to start? (emphasis added)

He also sets a therapeutic optimism by normalizing events the client had defined as abnormal or pathological. Most of the time, he accomplishes this by implication. The following example, however, is a time he did it on the explicit level. The client had been talking of the shamefulness of a previous period in her life when she was using drugs and was sexually promiscuous.

C: I've done it all—gotten married and got involved in drugs.
L: . . . then they're a prime target to become a victim of a mental health hierarchy. . . give them a label. . . so, in a way, you're grappling with a really human condition. . . So it turns the focus on whether or not you should be the target of your disgust or *this situation that we're all in.* (emphasis added)

Most of his normalizing, however, is on the implicit level. For example, Joan has just made an apology for not being able to show Lankton pictures of her son because she had put them in a purse that was later stolen.

*L:* I threw my wallet away in an Ace Hardware bag once...tossed it out with...a whole bunch of my pictures like that too.
(Here, his normalizing is combined with a one-down position; i.e., "I've goofed too.")

Scattered throughout the interview are comments in which Lankton reframes (redefines) a "negative" as a "positive." Again, such steps convey to the client that she is not dealing with exceptional deficits in her makeup, that there are more assets to her nature than she has realized. Referring to her preparing to "fall apart" near the end of her son's anticipated visit:

*C:* I'm already preparing...not to deal with it very well.
*L:* Does that work out? Do you *succeed* 100 percent of the time...? (emphasis added)

This is a beautiful "Ericksonian" framing: falling-apart symbolizes success; failure is the inability to fall apart, a "failure" representing a different strength within the client. At another point in the session, he has asked Joan if she continues to work part-time when her son is visiting. Her reply may have surprised him, since she continues to work at a full-time job, as well as at an extra job on most evenings. This could tempt therapists to point out the inconsistency between her concern about not having been a fulfilling mother and being so busy during his visit. Lankton, instead, turns her busyness into an asset.

*L:* ...that could be pretty nice because it gives him a chance to see you interacting in (many) ways and to model a nice person.

Another element contributing to the success of this session is the therapist's avoidance of conflict, that is, not arguing with the client. This is not as easy as it seems. Much traditional and current therapy relies on "confronting the client," often in a head-on manner, pointing out "false" or "mistaken" notions and the like. With little exception (for example, when challenging a client to take a beneficial step), it is extremely useful to avoid a conflictual stance; mostly, it keeps the therapy focus on resolving the stated problem without distracting the client into a struggle with the therapist. Lankton avoids conflict in a number of ways, mainly by expressing ideas in an equivocal fashion. The following example illustrates it in a very brief sentence utilizing *three* equivocations.

*L:* I wouldn't say it's "falling apart" you know . . . I would *think* it *might* be
   *maybe* "sad" . . . (emphasis added)

His comments are often qualified with "maybe," "probably," "I think,"
"might," "you could" (instead of "you will"), "sort of," and "but." The last
half of the session is implicitly defined as, "You're in a trance," and here
he is less equivocal. Framing an interaction with the client as a "trance" (or
"hypnosis") affords the therapist a maneuverability less available in the
ordinary course of therapy conversation, and especially the way in which
Lankton goes about it. He can afford to be more explicit, more directive,
in a context of "make believe" or "let's pretend," and all the more so since,
earlier in the session, he had defined the trance as one in which Joan would
be free "to sort out" what the therapist said was "relevant" for her and what
was not, and he acknowledged that he would be saying things that weren't
relevant. It's a sort of blanket understanding of, "If you don't see it the way
I put it, don't take it seriously."
   At some points he quite clearly veers away from a tack he's taken when
Joan indicates disagreement with it. He then simply agrees with her
viewpoint:

*C:* (Referring to her mother's death when Joan was three years old.) I mean
   it's hard for me to remember what she looked like . . . and I do remember
   a few things but I can't visualize her . . .
*L:* I can't . . . picture my mother, and she died fairly recently . . . that's
   probably the common thing . . .
*C:* Yeah, but three was young, I mean . . .
*L:* Three is definitely the worst scenario because you really need to have
   her around when you're three.

There was one segment in the interview in which Lankton, surprisingly,
departed from this kind of maneuverable stance. Just before the trance
work, he shifted to a one-up argumentative position. (Since he is an
extremely adept and sensitive therapist, I can only assume that he made
this mistake deliberately, out of compassion for the rest of us, who, all too
often, find ourselves enmeshed in quarrels with our clients.) Joan had just
validated his normalizing her earlier "weaknesses" and frailties, but she is
still bothered that she can't be firm enough in applying it to herself.

*L:* The part that doesn't make sense is that you unfortunately still are
   willing to think, "Maybe there's something wrong with me . . ." So while
   you kind of agree with what I'm saying . . . you start feeling so crummy
   you don't reach out and "people don't want to be around me."
*C:* Yeah, but I feel that sometimes I do it for the wrong (reason).

And later:

L: Why do you think you have to have a nervous breakdown . . . ? To be complete?

C: No, it's like, let me get it over with and then I'll be fine for the rest of my life.

L: Where did you get this idea that there's a nervous breakdown in the box that has to be? It doesn't say that in the instruction manual.

C: Well, . . . I'm recovering too from drugs and alcohol, and I have had a couple of setbacks in the past year and a half.

Arguing usually invites the client to justify her position, as in the above dialogue, continuing in an unresolved loop. Lankton finally breaks out of the loop by raising a rhetorical but useful question:

C: But it's so negative. Mother's Day . . . I'm the mother of a beautiful son, and I was depressed Mother's Day . . . and I fight with myself. . . ."

L: When was the last time you practiced feeling proud and happy?

C: I can't remember (laughing).

With this affirmation by Joan, Lankton builds on this theme: you have a right to be proud, but you experience depression since you don't practice feelings of motherly pride, and most worthwhile things require practice. With that, he shifts into the framing of "trance" which occupies the latter half of the session. Since Joan had mentioned that she had pictures of her son that she could bring to his office, Lankton uses that vehicle for "trance induction."

A word about "trance" and "hypnosis"—my using quotes means that I have reservations about those terms. They arose from and reflect a monadic or intrapsychic model, but are logically inconsistent with a systemic or interactional model, and thus the quotation marks. I have yet to find an appropriate alternative term to describe what I view as a conversation in which the role of the "hypnotist" is to do most of the talking and that of the "subject" is to listen; further, there is a procedure for negotiating "acceptable" comments between the parties. In Ericksonian style, these comments are most often phrased in qualified or ambiguous terms, allowing for error correction by the subject via yes responses ("Uh-huh" . . . "Yes," for example, and/or behavioral indicators, nodding or some physical compliance with a suggestion, such as, "You may find your hand wanting to lift") or via a non-yes response ("No," or a frown or non-compliance with a suggestion). Ambiguity and the use of implicit messages allows the "hypnotist" to shift to different framing if a non-yes response is elicited. The goal of this kind of interchange, as in all therapy conversations, is to elicit from the "subject" some acknowledgment of a desired change in viewpoint or, concretely, in the "subject's" behavior. As in much of Ericksonian psychotherapy, imagery, metaphor, analogy, and parable are commonly used forms of implication.

Lankton suggests to Joan that she regress to her own childhood, and, within that framing, he creates an imagined dialogue between that child and Joan. What follows is a complex series of imageries, but all interweaving the central theme: when you are feeling depressed or anxious, you don't have to experience that helplessly; you can use a procedure to reframe those feelings by imagining that you care for the child who was you and that child's principal need is that you feel good about yourself. For example:

*L:* Imagine making a deal or a trade of some kind happen when you feel something in your heart or feel something in your stomach that indicates she's signaling you that she has a need for that mother..."

And earlier:

*L:* Make a little trade that you each benefit from...Here's what it is. You be the mother who's proud and amazed and sad and tender and happy and loving and caring if she can be the little girl for you to provide continuity that you need on that side of the equation.

He makes the procedure more explicit:

*L:* And *rehearse* making that trade so that you can *have these resources available* at those times in the next few days and weeks and *years to come.* (emphasis added)

In essence, he is offering a procedure to Joan to enable her to get out of a counterproductive loop when she is feeling sufficiently "psychologically" uncomfortable. That Lankton was able to achieve this in one session is impressive.

Using different framing, imageries, and the like, he repeats that central theme:

*L:* But it does that child so much good to know that she was able to bring such joy to an adult. And maybe that's the greatest service we can provide to those children: to let them know, "You're valuable. It's important that you're here."

And, by analogy:

*L:* A lot of times my little girl has lost control by giggling. And she gets me giggling so hard that we start giggling about the fact that we're giggling.

He also varies the repetition through metaphor, as when he relates a story told by another client who discovers that what had originally been a nightmare was a lifesaving message from the past.

Finally, Lankton terminates the "trance" by having the client confirm that "something important happened," and follows that up by directly and explicitly reinforcing the procedure developed in the "trance."

*L:* How long a time do you think you had your eyes closed? (noncommittal query; author)

*C:* About 10 or 15 minutes. ("yes" response, since it was much longer; author)

*L:* It must have been about. . . a little over an hour, maybe close to an hour 15, 20 minutes. (unequivocal declaration of "time distortion"; author)

*C:* I felt like I was going to stay there.

*L:* Well, I guess you're going to practice that. I guess that's your sign that there was some useful material that you want to practice.

*C:* Oh, yeah. God!

As things come to a closure of the session, Lankton makes a final reframing redefining Joan's comment that the problem might still be current to "it's in the past":

*C:* I think I'm certainly going to practice that, you know. Because in the beginning I felt really sad and depressed, actually.

*L:* In the past, you *used to feel* depressed, huh? (emphasis added)

A final comment: In addition to all the things that Lankton did in this session, and on which I have already commented, he also used repetition. Over and over again, he makes the same point, utilizing varying forms of framing. It is something that may be more feasible in the "trance" context since, in the ordinary therapy conversation, repetition runs the risk of being seen as pedantic, or even condescending. In any case, repetition certainly did not hurt here, and was probably one of the strategic ingredients in a remarkably rapid success.

## References

Fisch, R., Weakland, J., & Segal, L. (1982). *The tactics of change: Doing therapy briefly.* San Francisco: Jossey-Bass.

Watzlawick, P., Weakland, J., & Fisch, R. (1974). *Change: Principles of problem formation and problem resolution.* New York: Norton.

# "Trance-formational" Moments in the Trance Work of a Session Conducted by Stephen R. Lankton

## Bradford P. Keeney, Ph.D., and Gregg Eichenfield, Ph.D.

In the clinical case of a woman with chronic anxiety and panic attacks, Stephen Lankton provides what he calls a "first and only session of brief therapy." Since the details of the case are given elsewhere in this monograph, we will only note that the beginning of Lankton's session is principally concerned with the setting forth of a range of topics, issues, and concerns, including the woman's anxiety, her making peace with her parental role, death in her family, drug use, relationship, and solitude.

With this initial elicitation of information, Lankton moves the case toward hypnotic work. This shift takes place when the woman is asked to close her eyes and create specific visualizations. At this point, the rest of the session breaks from the original thrust of a dialogue largely centered on gathering background information to a hypnotic situation in which the client receives suggestions from the therapist. Our comments attend to this trance work.

We invited several groups of experienced therapists with different backgrounds and areas of expertise to examine a transcript of the trance work of this case. For each page of transcript, the therapists were asked to identify what they believed might be possible moments of transformation.

The authors would like to thank Nancy Ankeny, Michael Bettendorf, Pamela Beyer, Maureen Campian, Linda Carole, MaryAnn Cincotta, Janice Colwill, Donna DiMenna, John Dwyer, Michael Earhart, Mary Frey, Jacquelin Germain, Vaughn Jefferson, Jr., Jane Klein, Janice Maidman, David Mathews, Deborah Miller, Sally Moore, Patricia Mullen, Maxine West, Rya Wiger, Timothy Wright, and Dan Yanisch for their many contributions to this study.

Address correspondence to Bradford P. Keeney, Ph.D., Dept. of Professional Psychology, University of St. Thomas, St. Paul, MN 55105-1096.

We provided no specific definition or discussion of "transformational moments" other than facilitating a consensual agreement that these moments concern the turning points at which therapeutic change may have taken place. Our preliminary findings indicate that different clinicians, even with varying backgrounds, more often than not find the same moments of transformation in a session.

In this case, we typically found certain conversational lines being used to set up a transformational moment. For instance, in the beginning of Lankton's trance work, he asks the woman to make internalized pictures of her son, beginning with when he was three years old and moving toward his present age. As she creates these pictures, she is asked to notice the feelings of pride and happiness associated with a mother's watching the development of her child.

By referring to those times that make a mother say, "Oh God, he's cool," and by the mention of smiles, laughter, and tenderness, a collection of resourceful experiences is brought forth. This set of experiences is then named as representing the same theme, that of "pride in being a mother."

The moment of classifying these resourceful associations as the "pride of a mother" is the first major transformational moment in the session's trance work. With this major resourceful theme, the therapist asks the client to picture herself growing up from age three while juxtaposing the previously scanned pictures of her son. She is instructed to hold onto the good feelings associated with being a mother.

At this time, the therapist quickly shifts to having the client become aware of her body, noting the difference between tension and relaxation. Relaxation is connoted as an indication of good feelings. This not only sets up the woman to be aware of good feelings in a present state condition, but also indirectly enables her to connect body relaxation with the theme of a mother's pride.

The trance work moves back to having the woman view herself as a three-year-old while carrying the positive feelings of a caring mother (now linked to the association of a relaxed body). This leads to the most significant transformational moment in the session, when communication is suggested between the woman's image of herself as a three-year-old and the image of herself as a grown-up in a way that is resourceful to both the child and the grown-up. In this bartering setup, each temporal image helps the other, providing the woman with an inner therapeutic chamber in which to work on her problems and issues. The grown-up image, with its gifts of protection and caring, is available to the child image, with its gifts of happiness and joy. In exchanges of "happiness," each is able to give to the other what may be missing in another spatial/temporal reality.

The next major transformational moment involved reframing the woman's "anxiety" as a vibration that could be associated with "giggling."

The vibrations of an adult's anxiety could then be exchanged for the vibrations of her inner child's giggling.

Having brought the inner bartering meditation as a resource for handling the presenting complaint of anxiety, the therapist proceeds to demonstrate how a wide range of difficulties can be addressed. In this stage of the trance work, most of the woman's original complaints are worked within the inner therapeutic bartering chamber.

A final transformational moment involved the masterful mention of the presence of her mother's spirit. A story about a possibly "real" ghost involving another person's son in a three-generational context helped to underscore the existentially real presence of her mother's absence. With this idea in place, it was suggested that the daughter might live to bring her mother peace. This transformation potentially shifts the focus off of the woman's complaints and moves her to helping others through conduct that happens to be most resourceful to her own development.

The identification of transformational moments in this case helps recapture the dramaturgical essence of therapy. Seen as a genre of theatrical performance, the mastery and mystery of a great case are inextricably linked to the turning points that move the therapeutic story through its labyrinth. The aesthetic skills required to pull this off, that is, to make it a believable reality, heavily rely upon the subtle and often indirect maneuverings to set up a turning point or moment of transformation. In all these regards, Lankton's work is a superb example of the resourceful theater of the therapeutic.

In closing, we offer several questions regarding the further evolution of the "inner bartering therapeutic chamber."

1. Can an "inner mediator" be created whose job it is to negotiate resourceful exchanges successfully?
2. Can an "inner history" of successful mediations in the bartering chamber enable a client to hand over the job to the mediator, giving up conscious awareness of future work in the chamber?
3. How may the juxtaposed evolutions and devolutions of the woman's inner images repeat themselves, becoming an endless karmic process of recycled autobiography?
4. May these recycled choreographies between the "past present" and "present future" be sped up temporarily or accelerated so as to perpetually create new unities and identities?
5. Do clients with such internalized realities retain the therapist's voice? Or is this voice masked behind other voices? Does the therapist become the voice of the architect/builder of the inner chamber? of the mediator? of the clock setter? of the woman? of the whispering of Godot? of the silence or silencing of presenting absences?

# Trickster Coyote Meets the February Mother: A Commentary on Lankton's Case Transcript

## Lynn D. Johnson, Ph.D.

As we examine this case, our challenge is to create an explanation for the good outcome. Since follow-up suggests that this patient, who was having frequent anxiety attacks before this treatment, no longer has such attacks, has made some positive changes in her life, and seems symptom-free, how are we to account for that? Something presumably has happened during therapy that orients the patient away from symptoms and toward a more empowered style of life. Since there are various points of view on this, and since the case is full of many subtleties and interventions, I will confine myself to one simple observation, and let others with greater insight fill in what I overlook.

During the first half of this case, Lankton is occasionally irrelevant, stumbling, almost inarticulate. Later he becomes fluent and polished, and we see the Lankton thumbprint — a series of linked ideas whose organization is extraordinarily complex and which Lankton keeps in his head like a memorized periodic table of the elements.

Why do we see these two, opposite styles? Is that just an artifact (he is slow to warm up and get going), or is there some method here? Is there any advantage to looking less fluent than one really is? Could it be that a bumbling style early in the session facilitates a more complete response to hypnosis?

It seems to me that perhaps there is a real danger in the therapist/ hypnotist's appearing to be too competent and able. Perhaps the obvious competence allows or invites the patient to be less involved, to be too passive and uninvolved, like when riding in a car with someone very

Address correspondence to Lynn D. Johnson, Ph.D., Ste. B-108, 166 E. 5900 South, Salt Lake City, UT 84107.

competent, you don't pay much attention to where you are going, but if the driver appears to be on the edge of being completely lost, you pull out a map and try harder to help.

And this is the sense we get when we watch Lankton in this case. He seems to be lost early on, at least part of the time, stumbling for words, searching for explanations; as the session matures, he begins to flow quite effortlessly.

I remember quite clearly my first impression of Erickson. I had written to him about my experiences in learning hypnosis, and he was kind enough to reply and to encourage me to continue. When I asked if he would let me watch him work to learn from him, he agreed, and I went with great expectations. However, during my first day with him, he did not seem like a sage at all. Instead, he pulled out cartoons he had clipped from the papers, and showed them to us. The common theme was one of multiple meanings in language, but as he laughed almost manically at jokes he had obviously seen over and over, the thought occurred to me, "I am too late! His mind has already gone. The man is senile." Later that day, and in subsequent work with him, I realized that this, like other of my first impressions, was an error. He was as senile as a wily fox, as incompetent as the legendary coyote. Just when I thought I had figured him out, there would be a twist and I would be lost again.

So what do we see but a quintessential trickster, the coyote who pretends to be lame to win the contest, the palace jester who is the only one who can tell the king the truth. I decided after a while that part of Erickson's genius was his unpretentiousness: he was quite willing to appear to be a fool or a jester if it would help me learn. And I wonder if I hear an echo of this as Lankton mutters incoherently or struggles to find words.

I don't claim that Lankton has thought this through, although I wouldn't put it past him. For years he has been the master of the personal aside, an irrelevant "throwaway" comment apparently muttered absentmindedly to himself, but which serves as a punch line to a joke, or as a tag line to make memorable some idea or point. He may have developed this jester style unconsciously by responding to the cues clients would give him. He may have noticed that the confused style elicited a more complete response from clients than did a confident, "Now look at that spot on the wall and notice that your eyes are getting heavy heavy heavy, and you are going deeper deeper and still deeper deeper into blah blah land." He may have had the same irreverent thought that I had about Erickson's apparent senile dementia, which would mysteriously clear up just at a crucial time. Or maybe he is just lucky.

I don't think all of this confusion is some pacing of the client, since Lankton actually opens the session with some autistic comments about his nose and ears and having flown in from Pensacola, sort of the opposite of the usual opening in which we are terribly concerned about and focused only on the patient. And traditional views of the therapy relationship would suggest that Lankton here makes a technical error, that he contaminates the relationship with such a self-referential statement. The results in the case belie that idea. The patient seems deeply involved in the procedure, and immediate and follow-up results suggest a beautiful utilization of the ideas Lankton offers her.

The patient complains of anxiety attacks and links them to an idea that she could disappear and it wouldn't matter, that her life is not meaningful. While Lankton's initial thought is that she doesn't have any aggressive, distancing behaviors available to her, she says, "Yes, but." She explains this feeling of anxiety, which is about falling apart by experiencing despair that comes from the early loss of her mother when the patient was three, the loss of her son to his father's custody when the son was four, and the fact that she was using alcohol and drugs, and of her life not being important. However, she does have positive and proud feelings about her son.

The idea of hypnosis was seeded early in the session, so Lankton simply begins to work at a hypnotic level. As is typical for him, he does almost nothing to "induce" a trance, working minimally to induce her to think in a reflective, inward way. Lankton follows her lead into a pattern of linking the present positive feelings she has for her son (using a serendipitous account of how her purse was stolen and she thus lost some important pictures of him from the age of three to age nine or ten). He asks her to imagine looking at those pictures and to respond to the feelings she has, enjoying feelings of being a proud mother watching her son grow. Then she continues to hold onto those feelings, using an anchor of a wrist squeeze, and begins to see some pictures of herself as a three-year-old. She is having feelings of being a proud mother and seeing pictures of herself. She holds onto the proud-mother feelings, sees herself, and then Lankton suggests a trade. The adult self trades a feeling of a good mother who is proud of the child part and interested in her, and the child gives that mother a feeling that she is needed and wanted and important. And there will be a particular ideosensory response whenever that child inside wants to feel the care and interest of the mother she didn't have, and the woman who feels unneeded can feel a sense of being needed by that internal child. Like Erickson's famous "February man" cases, her history (memory and meaning) changes, but instead of doing so through a relationship with Lankton, it is through a relationship with herself.

The patient becomes her own mother, a proxy mother to the sense of loss as a child. The adult self can feel a positive sense of needing/being needed on a regular basis, something that will substitute for the empty feeling and the lack of connection and involvement in her current life. The work is well done, and I suggest that the interested reader track these ideas through the whole therapy transcript.

She has a very positive response to this intervention. She feels comfortable and relaxed and very optimistic. Follow-up reports that Lankton received are that she has not had any further anxiety attacks. She has terminated a dead-end relationship (that had lasted for years), and has begun more positive relationships. She has not had further counseling. She said that she was going to call for an appointment, but decided she did not need to do that.

Since this is a profound change, it challenges us to understand what happened. If we simply were to suggest that the woman pretend to be her own mother/child and feel needed and nurtured by needing and nurturing herself, she would be unlikely to end a long relationship with anxiety based on that suggestion. The therapy process must be enchanting and entrancing, not dry and intellectual. She must alter her basic meanings and understanding, something hypnosis facilitates. And that hypnosis must be an active, involved process for her, not something she sits back and lets happen. So my point is that this Lieutenant Colombo routine of Lankton's may have facilitated such a deep involvement, in that since she didn't expect much, she is more likely to flow along with the process than if she came in with high expectations.

While I have often been skeptical that we mere mortals can do the complex, multiple embedded metaphors that Lankton loves to do, this is a pattern I can endorse for all therapists: Act dumb and carry a smart stick.

# The Healing Power of the Story

## Carol J. Kershaw, Ed.D.

Story is medicine (Estes, 1992). The story has the healing power to allow a person to reorganize internal categories and retrieve resources that are needed for whole functioning. Stephen Lankton's one-session case demonstrates how "restorying" (Kershaw, 1992)—that is, working with the patient's story with deep empathy and hypnotic narrative to write a new story—can create a holding environment, use emotional arousal, and provide new associations to a historical story that has deadened its narrator.

The patient's story is one of loss, sadness, mourning, and yearning. Joan's mother died when Joan was three, her grandmother died when Joan was 11, her father was alcoholic, and because of her own alcohol and drug problems, her ex-husband was awarded custody of her son. She feels unseen, unknown, and unmothered, as though she matters to no one. She suffers from anxiety, panic attacks, and disconnection to a loving community or companion. She expects to have an emotional breakdown in the near future, but deeply yearns for connection to herself and her son. This lost woman demonstrates how she has been culturally induced to believe the story about her. Gilbert and Gubar (1979) suggest that "women will starve in silence until new stories are created which confer on them the power of naming themselves."

One of the characters in Virginia Woolf's *Between the Acts* says, "It is time someone wrote a new plot." Lankton begins to assist Joan in cowriting a new story line by connecting with her as a parent and reinforcing how she can develop more personal authority and power. Her past must be renamed, and be given a new perspective. But the mind does not easily relinquish remorse.

The patient mourns the loss of her own childhood, her own son, and her self. Lankton connects with her empathically, and begins to educate her on how to talk to her son about the divorce; he describes to her the way

Address correspondence to Carol J. Kershaw, Ed.D., Milton H. Erickson Institute, 2012 Bissonnet, Houston, TX 77005.

in which children quietly react to such discussions with little response, but in the future come back for deeper connection. He suggests that she begin with, "You know that Mommy loves you," an embedded suggestion about her own mother's love. Lankton tells the story of a son who, after years of listening to derogatory comments about his dad, concluded that his mother must have had emotional conflict and that his father had value. The son breaks his silence, and finally tells his father. Lankton suggests to Joan that she feel anger at the inequality of having perceptions of one parent filtered through the anger of another. It is difficult to correct distortions and mis-understandings, but children begin to develop their own perceptions. He assures her that her son one day will step out of the spell created by her ex-husband. In the meantime, rather than having a breakdown, it would seem a better idea to take a refreshing break out of a negative state of consciousness that a vacation could provide.

Lankton focuses on the change in affect that this woman needs: the ability to feel pride and happiness in herself. He begins to elicit this re-source from her as she reviews in her imagination the pictures of her own child at different ages. She has lost the wallet pictures of him, which symbolizes her connection with her biological child and her own child within. Lankton encourages Joan to recognize that connections can be remembered and reviewed in the imagination. Then he asks her to hold these feelings while she reviews pictures of herself, and so give herself all the pride and joy she feels for her own son. She becomes her own mother and Lankton is her symbolic father who suggests self-mothering in trance. Lankton focuses on the early developmental task that was left unaccom-plished – that of learning basic trust and being appropriately mirrored for self-esteem. He helps her repair the connection between her dead mother and herself, and suggests that she replace anxiety with giggling. Rather than falling apart emotionally, she could "fall apart" into laughter.

Through metaphor and story, Lankton breaks the old dysfunctional trance in which Joan functions. He offers new possibilities through the construction of a new story for herself that has power and heart. The holding environment is established between Joan as her own mother, the connection is reinforced positively with her biological mother, and Lankton is the symbolic father.

While Lankton expresses empathy and co-writes a new story with Joan's unconscious, he uses emotional arousal and cognitive disorganization to stimulate the patient's receptivity to an important change in attitude. The research literature suggests that when a client genuinely feels cared for, anxiety can be tolerated and channeled toward change. Eventually, the old feelings and provocations no longer trigger the same negative state of consciousness. The voice and the face of the therapist act as a holding environment and bridge to new interpretations and experiences. She can feel joy and pride in herself, establish a reconnection with her son, and begin to live more functionally.

Madness results when a person's life story is drained of vitality so that it shrinks and shrivels through being disconfirmed, discounted, demeaned, and controlled. Lankton helps Joan develop a new past story that is victimless and has more flexibility and a future narrative that is positive and achievable, by suggesting specific behaviors to create them. He suggests through hypnotic narrative a new plot and story line for her to take control of her own life. He praises her for being female, and suggests that she is valuable by sharing stories of his delight in his own daughter. Since she received little confirmation from her own mother, who left prematurely through death, and from her father, who left emotionally, she receives reparenting from Lankton and is taught how to give herself internal soothing.

Change occurs for Joan because she learns how to forgive and nurture herself, and perhaps the most powerful shift takes place when Lankton ends his ghost story by suggesting, "Maybe, in some way, that spirit of your mother has been satisfied in realizing that you hit upon a way that frees her now to rest in peace knowing that the little girl that she abandoned can bring a smile to the face of her mother, who really needs a smile brought to her face by a child on a regular basis." Lankton implies that Joan can allow her mother peace by her comforting her own internal child from the "mother" aspect of herself.

As people progress through different developmental stages and spiral processes, there are developmental states of consciousness, as well as pathological states of consciousness, that are encoded as patterns of electrical activity. These states of consciousness have a certain organization of thought, a certain kind of awareness, and compulsory and rigid behavior, and can be triggered in a variety of ways. Before the hypnotic intervention, Joan seemed to find herself consistently in a negative state of consciousness with no known passageway to the outside.

Lankton provided the healing trance with Joan. The healing trance is a state of focused attention in which unconscious minds meet and a more positive identity is storied by the therapist so that the patient experiences a change in belief, perspective, and self-narrative. His voice, as well as the trance itself, provides a "holding environment" to cradle Joan and nurture her through a reorganization of self-distortion to a more positive identity. In his last hypnotic narrative, Lankton suggests to Joan that if she finds herself reviewing the negative, she can skip from one negative word to a positive one. The implication is that Joan has so much more power than she thinks.

Story is medicine for the unconscious. The unconscious is mother/father to the adult who has lost soul, who has fears of making new connections, of humiliation, of being someone. The hypnotic narrative can restory a mind (Kershaw, 1992), and as Lankton demonstrates so well, can restore hope for the future.

# References

Estes, C. (1992). *Women who run with the wolves: Myths and stories of the wild woman archetype*. New York: Ballantine Books.

Gilbert, S., & Gubar, S. (1979). *The mad woman in the attic*. New Haven: Yale University Press.

Kershaw, C. (1991). *The couple's hypnotic dance*. New York: Brunner/Mazel.

Kershaw, C. (1992). Restorying the mind: Evoking the healing trance. Paper delivered to the Fifth International Ericksonian Congress, Phoenix, Ariz.

# Comment on Therapy by Stephen Lankton, M.S.W.: Case of a Woman with Chronic Anxiety and Panic Attacks

## Betty Alice Erickson, M.S., L.P.C.

This is an excellent example of therapy being accomplished within one brief session. After just a single visit, the client felt secure, confident, and, in her words, "reempowered." Her chronic and acute anxiety became manageable. These changes have endured and continued for over a year. The successes of this very brief interaction are due to a number of reasons, not the least of which is the skill of Lankton.

Although both Lankton and the client focused on her immediate life, Lankton was able to address indirectly unresolved issues in her past. She not only obtained new parenting skills and relief of her anxiety about parenting issues, but she also was able to use coming to peace with her past as a method of continuing to learn to parent her son well.

A number of interventions were used. There seemed to be no one interaction, no one turning point, that can be extracted and pointed to as the moment when the client incorporated changes. As Lankton talked to his client, he carefully built upon her perceived strengths, as well as on previous statements. He braided together new patterns of perception, ability, and options for the client to use.

However, the use of hypnosis, in my opinion, was the main underpinning of the successful outcome. The trance state enabled the client to tap into her unconscious resources to recognize her abilities, to nurture herself, and to use both past experiences and her current life situation to manage her anxiety attacks and her despair.

Address correspondence to Betty Alice Erickson, M.S., L.P.C., 3710 Rawlins, Suite 1065, Dallas, TX 75219.

Lankton first developed the trance state naturalistically by asking the client to close her eyes "for just a minute and see if you can picture that series of photographs. . . ." Later Lankton built on that internal focus of remembering and developed a more formal trance, which he directed in specific directions.

An analysis of this session reveals a number of ways in which Lankton was able to help his client. Obviously, she was ready to change, or, at least, was very willing to try to change. She was tired of her anxiety and despair. Lankton took this willingness at face value and expected good results. The overall ambiance of the session was that of success.

He did an excellent job of joining with Joan as a friendly, nonauthoritative person who had some interesting and useful information for her. As he explained the checklist of personality characteristics, he gave examples of dominant and competent behavior, which was behavior she had displayed—everyone has dealt with a telemarketing call; every parent has told a child to sit down. He then slipped in a reasonable explanation for at least a piece of her anxiety: dominant and disaffiliative behaviors from someone who did not believe that she had these abilities were anxiety provoking.

Her agreement that she did have some of those behaviors opened the door to further change. The first change a client accomplishes is often a metaphor for further change. An "I never looked at it that way" can be the basis for further changes in perspectives that allow additional options.

Lankton used humor with the client—only so many shopping days left to falling apart. Most clients have little humor in their lives and take themselves far too seriously. The ability to laugh at problems not only is healthy, but is a tool that can be used throughout life. Lankton continued to use humor throughout the session. At one point, a joke enabled him to reinforce appropriate behavior, as well to compliment her in a way with which she could not disagree: "Maturing takes all the fun out of those crummy things." At another point, he joked with her about her lack of practice in feeling proud and happy in a way that enabled her to understand that she was in control of more of her emotions than she thought she was. She also was able to realize that sometimes she did practice good emotions, which then set up a framework for the conscious continuation of this.

The client had legitimate anxiety about the parenting of her son. Lankton gave her a way in which to be an effective parent, and structured it so that she wouldn't be disappointed if she didn't see immediate results. She did need to tell her son why his father had custody of him. Then Lankton carefully structured a way for the client to terminate this difficult discussion with an easily pictured example of an "offstage line."

This was a magnificent multilevel communication which simply had to work. Imagining the reaction of an audience to an overheard final offstage line of an entertainer after a performance is an intriguing and almost irresistible thought. Turning inward to think and imagine sets up a naturalistic trance. Thus, possible defenses are breached and the subject is able to consider and accept information that might be ignored or rejected in the ordinary waking state.

Acceptance that the *manner* of communication not only can be the most important part of the message, but can convey an unspoken attitude in a memorable way, is a thought that can be debated verbally. A naturalistic trance allows that information to be considered and compared with life experiences without that conscious debate. This information, received in a naturalistic trance state, also allowed the client to recognize that she could control the manner of delivery. Therefore, she could control a great deal of the impact of the information on her son.

Lankton then shifted the cadence of his speech to a more normal conversational tone as he began an unnecessary buttressing of his information. Perhaps, however, this was his way of ending the trance state in a manner that would invite her to begin focusing on another issue.

Lankton then moved into a more formal hypnotic trance with the client. He suggested that she hold onto feelings of joy and pleasure that parents have, and picture herself as a child, as a three-year-old, all the while maintaining the feelings of a caring mother. The directions were very specific and clear, while allowing the client to define the feelings in a way that fit within her.

The purpose of this trance was to have the client "mother" herself so that she would heal the loss of the mothering she never received. That goal was clearly laid out when Lankton told her that "even though it may have sort of occurred to her that she was never going to know how proud mothers felt about a child, . . . you are a proud mother feeling that way about her right now."

This was a nice circular construction: as a motherless child, she would feel the loss of a mother's pride; as a mother, she felt a mother's pride; and she could feel that same pride as she looked at herself as a child, which would then let that child have a mother who felt pride. She could nurture and comfort herself as she thought about herself as a child. In a trance, the giving of love to herself as a child was pleasing. Recognition of that pleasure not only was nurturing to herself as an adult, but was a legitimate trade-off for the giving of that love to herself as a child.

Additionally, this framework helped her recognize that the loss of mothering to herself was significant, just as the loss of her daily mothering is significant to her son. Recognition of the significance of that loss of daily mothering would enable her to understand that she is important to her son—that it would indeed affect him more than marginally if she "fell off the face of the earth."

The unconscious operates in a childlike concrete way. It is important to respect that way of thinking. It is not "fair" to give a child something, even if that something is love and protection and caring, without receiving "something" back. It is adult thinking to recognize that the pleasure of seeing a child grow and flourish is more than enough payment.

To a child, the loss of a mother is a tremendous blow. While she was in the trance, Lankton addressed his obvious belief that this loss had had a strong effect on his client. He talked about the three-year-old's sadness and the client's adult sadness for herself as a child who had lost her mother. He then did a neat flip and suggested that the mother had been deprived of the joys of watching the client grow to adulthood. This was followed by the suggestion that now the spirit, the ghost, of her mother could be at peace. He finished with a story about a ghost, even though he discounted the story by saying that he didn't believe in ghosts.

A major reason for this session's success was that Lankton used hypnosis so skillfully. He not only enabled the client to tap into her unconscious resources and her learned experiences in a positive way, but he also used the trance state to give her specific instructions in a very open framework. He had her link her remembered and imagined childhood with her adult abilities and wisdom. This blending was done on an experiential level that was reached through hypnosis.

Even though most of the work was done while the client was in a trance, Lankton taught her specific behaviors, which gave her the conscious security of guidelines. The really important work and resolutions did not have to surface prematurely in order to satisfy the normal desire for instructions to help overcome problems. These instructions were tagged with humor and intensified by the analogy of the offstage line.

The humor Lankton displayed was very important. While never deprecating her fears and problems, it clearly carried the message that life can be enjoyable and that almost anything can provide amusement. When one enjoys life and knows how to find pleasure, one has a life foundation upon which problems rest less threateningly and so become less overwhelming.

In the wrap-up of the session, Lankton could not resist one last metaphorical hammering down of what the client had learned. In his conversation about the dictionary on his computer, he said, "...we'd gone from this one set that was relatively negative and gone all the way to this other one, and I realized how...it was a good exercise...."

And indeed it was.

# Commentary on Lankton's Case

## Robert E. Pearson, M.D.

Milton Erickson sometimes told the ancient story of several blind men describing an elephant, each interpreting his findings on the basis of his own restricted tactile sensations and past experiences. Erickson would then add that all of the descriptions were correct, though incomplete, and that, in spite of it all, *the elephant remained an elephant.* Was the elephant changed because of that experience, as many would say? Very little, I feel, and that in only occasionally remembering that one day a number of strange men palpated various parts of an elephant's anatomy at the same time, and then argued about something, each seeming to believe that only he had arrived at the "truth."

Each of us commenting on or reading the various interpretations of this case should keep those observations in mind.

Any trained and experienced therapist interested enough to read the transcript of this case will have some ideas about why Lankton's approach worked so well, and all of his or her ideas are part of the truth. My comments will be centered around a few ideas that some may consider not very important, or possibly even trivial; I obviously believe that they played an important part in the success of the therapy.

First, the client was well prepared to receive help, and wanted it [*Editor's note:* Introductory material explained that she had not been seen for the previous four years. Until that time, she had been a client of another therapist for over a year.]. Remember that in spite of what they say, and for whatever reason people present themselves to a therapist, some really don't want to change, and others are afraid to. This woman was ready. She didn't like the way she had been behaving; a recurring crisis was only four weeks away, and she wanted to behave differently this time.

As part of the preparation for this session, the client was told (or at least probably interpreted whatever was actually said) that a famous expert

Address correspondence to Robert Pearson, M.D., 10044 Lynbrook Drive, Houston, TX 77042.

was being brought in from afar *just to see her*. This idea is confirmed by Lankton's first statement: "I'm from Pensacola, and I flew in, and my ear hasn't cleared, so when you see me blowing this ear here. . . . It's not a permanent thing I do; just temporary, for a couple of days after flying." I can almost hear her thinking, "He flew in here in bad weather just to see me." And at the end of the session, she asks if he is "heading home." He responds, "Yeah, tonight I will, if those thunderstorms don't stop me." Magnificent reinforcement! Incidentally, I wouldn't be surprised if this had provoked an amnesia for much of the session. One of the ways that Erickson taught us to induce an amnesia is to chat idly with a client about anything *but* the therapy issues, to deal with the problems at hand, and then to pick up again on the original idle chatter. The client will often "lose" conscious memory of the intervening subject(s).

Quite a bit of time was spent in dealing with how she had reacted in the past to the upcoming crisis (her son's summer visit) and how she would like to react, as well as her weaknesses in other areas (including men friends), but also the strengths she has had to function in other fields, such as her work. All of that was important, but in the interest of keeping this commentary within bounds, and to keep from repeating what is obvious, I shall go on.

Lankton refrained from belaboring the parallel between Joan's mother's death when Joan was three and Joan's "abandoning" her son when he was about the same age. Erickson, when dealing with bed-wetters, didn't talk about bladders; he talked about such things as learning to hit a pitched ball or to do other things better and better as time goes on. He didn't have to insult the children by saying, "In case you missed the point, I'm really talking about bladders." And so, too, with Lankton in this case; he refrains from hitting her on the head.

In responding to her comment, "I'm waiting to have the nervous break-down *I should have had* when my son was given to his father" (emphasis added), Lankton suggests that perhaps a breakdown here and now might be helpful. Beautiful! Shades of, "How much headache do you *need*?" Think of how the rest of the session might have gone if she had taken him up on the offer.

Shortly after that, a fascinating interchange takes place. She says, "It's like, let me get it over with (the nervous breakdown), and then I'll be fine for the rest of my life." Lankton responds (on the tape, he sounds irritated), "Where did you get this idea that there's a nervous breakdown in the box (of tools)? It doesn't say that in the instruction manual. Okay, lose child, go home, have a nervous breakdown, pick up parts, put them in the box."

In a voice that sounds as though she is trying to garner sympathy, she says, "Well, I think you know, I'm 'recovering' too from drugs and alcohol, and I have had a couple of setbacks in the past year and a-half." Lankton will have none of that. He says, "But you need to answer the question. Where did you get the idea? That's the predominant thing that keeps coming around. Where did you get the impression that that's part of the deal?" Only then does she back down, "It's just in my head where I feel like I just want to take a break from everything."

I believe that this was the turning point in the session. From that point on, Joan stayed in a trance and listened without verbal comment, while Lankton gave her very precise instructions on how to be a surrogate mother, first to herself, and then also to her son. Many pages could be written (and probably will be) about the dynamics involved, but I will refrain from that, except to say that I greatly admire how Lankton tailored the therapy to suit the client's needs, and that you cannot argue with success.

# Reflections on Stephen Lankton's Work with Joan

## Jane Parsons-Fein, CSWBCD

### Creative Artistry and Technical Skill

Lankton's work with Joan is a demonstration that the healing process that takes place on levels we call "unconscious" requires creative artistry as well as technical skill. The artist works with the complex in deceptively simple ways. In his work with a despairing and anxious mother who had lost her own mother when the client was three, and who was separated from her son by divorce when he was "almost four," Lankton quickly joins with her in her world. With gentle good humor, he guides her through a labyrinth of learning, moving with her through levels of experience with such a light touch that the depth of the impact on her might easily be missed, and indeed only becomes evident in the follow-up to this session 18 months later. In work with Ericksonian approaches, this is as it should be. Often it was years before some of the hypnotic seeds Erickson planted bore fruit.

Aristotle wrote: "In part, art completes what nature cannot elaborate... [Art] consists in bringing something into existence." Based on the follow-up feedback, this session with Lankton brought something into Joan's existence that nature hadn't elaborated. I think it was a series of creative moments elegantly generated and anchored into her physiology in holographic fashion.

Erickson's unique approach to hypnosis and trance was geared toward a growth process of the "disorganizing, reorganizing, reassociating, and projecting of inner real experience." (Erickson & Rossi, 1979, p. 9). His concept of "experiential life" was always anchored in the physiology, the sensory-motor system. He wrote about therapeutic hypnosis: "It is this

Address correspondence to Jane Parsons-Fein, CSWBCD, NYSEPH, 275 Central Park West, Apt. 4B, New York, NY 10024.

experience of reassociating and reorganizing his own experiential life that eventuates in a cure" and "the induction and maintenance of trance serve to provide a special psychological state in which the patient can achieve this inner resynthesis" (Erickson & Rossi, 1980, p. 461). In the same paper, Rossi writes of "creative moments in therapy," saying:

> A creative moment occurs when a habitual pattern of association is interrupted. . . . It is a gap in one's habitual pattern of awareness. . . . The new that appears in creative moments is thus the basic unit of original thought and insight as well as the generator of personality change. . . . Experiencing a creative moment may be the phenomenological correlate of a critical change in the molecular structure of proteins within the brain associated with learning (Gaito, 1972) or the creation of new cell assemblies and phase sequences (Hebb, 1963).

## The Creative Moment and Molecular Biology

There have been relevant discoveries in molecular biology. Candace Pert, Ph.D., is an internationally recognized pharmacologist who has published over 250 scientific articles about brain peptides and their receptors. In an interview I did with her last year, she talked about the physiological response to pattern interruption, which is what generates the creative moment (Parsons-Fein, 1992).

*Pert:* I think that this is the physical key to accessing this or that series of memories; you go in through a certain peptide substance, which is related to a certain emotional state. Depending on what mode you are in, you can switch from one kind of a memory to another.

*Parsons:* And that is what we try to do, intervene in that pattern and bring in another, I suppose what you would call, peptide. Sometimes you have to shock someone or sometimes pattern-interrupt to get them out of that place they are in.

*Pert:* Yes, they are in some loop. Their brain is saying, "Go from peptide A to B and then to D, go to A, go to B, go to D," and they are just flooded. And then I think they get some other peptide and then they are in a new mode, which might have insight. This is true; the evidence is already there.

It would seem that Pert is tracking on a molecular level the changes that are introduced when shifts of consciousness occur. Erickson said, "In hypnosis you are seeking to alter. . .the body's responses." It would also seem that the creative artistry of the hypnotherapist is in knowing how and when to "bring into existence" the new patterns to complete "what nature did not elaborate" – to, in effect, introduce new peptides.

In his work with Joan, Lankton moves with her changing states of consciousness as she becomes more and more relaxed and trusting, interrupting the flow at just the right moments to take the lead in shifting her into deeper and deeper states of creative awareness, culminating in an age regression/progression that has many levels and is exquisitely wrought.

## The Creative Moment and Pattern Interruption

Pattern interruption is one hypnotic technique that makes the creative moment possible. Erickson often said that the mind abhors a vacuum. "Always say the unexpected. When you say the unexpected, the other person has to rearrange his thinking." Following are a few of the many examples of this that are in the session: humor ("Yeah, maturing can take all the fun out of all those crummy things"); unexpected pacing ("Well, now's a good time [to have that nervous breakdown]. I've got 45 minutes"); a random observation taken out of context in response to her statement, "My choice is men sucks" ("Stand-up comic. There's a role for you"); seemingly unrelated phrase or metaphor, in response to her comment, "I was depressed Mother's Day" ("Well, then, how in the hell do you expect as the clock turns midnight and not even do what you practiced"); reframing ("I have a brother-in-law who's an expert guitarist and at midnight he could play classical guitar when the clock turned to 'Classical Guitarist Day' ") ("What a nice way to fall apart with people"); and my favorite reframe ("A nervous breakdown isn't an especially good break...Bimini is a much better idea. Bahamas is good").

As they begin the session, Lankton uses voice-tone changes; rhythm changes and marking; pattern interruption; expectation of the successful use of trance; constant reframing, which is often humorous; the anchor word "tools," which he intersperses throughout the session; and, in addition, her "ability to articulate" and her "dignity." He confuses her with concepts of irrelevancy/relevancy, and in the vacuum that results from confusion, reassures her of the relevancy of their talk together, a clear statement that she can grab hold of – like a life raft in the waters of her confusion. He then moves her to her anxiety and shifts to the expectation of success, again using alternative aspects of accomplishment. This effectively brings her to her "on-the-edge feeling" and the painful association to the death of her mother at an early age, and the replay of all the pain that her little-girl mind could not let her experience consciously.

## Pattern Shifting

Pattern shifting can include pattern interruption, reframing, transitioning, deepening, fractionation, metaphor, physical movement, change of rhythm, and a variety of nonverbal cues. I have a client who said to me one day: "I'm moving into a place where I'm not so engaged with my pain that I don't have a place for other people."

Here is an example early in the session after they explore "falling apart." Joan talks of breaking down and being torn up, and Lankton says, "You need to make peace with that somehow, with what your role is going to be with your son." Then he continues with a train of mental shifting:

> When...I got a little bit of familiarization with your history. Your husband got custody like when he was three or four, something like that. So, that would have been...what...he's 10, so seven years ago or so, seven or eight years ago. Well, gosh, you have...wait a minute (pattern interruption, seeding expectations) tell me about this...the goal here. The goal is to...(voice-tone change)...I think that may be helpful to...[the referring therapist] mentioned that you'd been... that she had done a session with you where you put yourself in a trance (experiential access) and found that to be a possibility (expectation access), and since I'm teaching professionals in hypnosis (Lankton in charge), it makes sense that that would be one of the tools (anchor) we would use for your anxiety. And since people put themselves in trance by basically putting themselves into a trance (confusion, recursion), the things that I say, if irrelevant, are totally irrelevant to the listener. So if I can be relevant, so much the better (confusion). And so talking about your son's coming up in a month is very relevant, I'm sure (clear statement), and if not now, will be soon (suggestion, reassurance). But I think I should hear some more from you about (shift) what do you think...when did all this anxiety start? I don't really...I've gotten the words from someone else, but if I can see it through your eyes, if you could fill me in on what you'd like to accomplish or what you think we could accomplish or anything not to accomplish, whatever, anything (all alternatives, open ended).

She comes quickly to her anxiety, her on-the-edge feeling, and associates that with her mother's death.

Another element of the hypnotherapeutic relationship is that the therapist and client move together through states of consciousness simultaneously as the therapist interrupts the pattern, directing them from one realm into another. There was complete consistent resonance between Lankton and Joan as she shifted from one state of consciousness to another, from one feeling to another, from one anchor to another, from one imprint to another, from one association to another, step by step toward the deepest age regression and profound reframe of the context of her relationship with her mother, her grandmother, herself, and, therefore, her son.

> "I constantly validate self-worth. I work on the
> process and the problems take care of
> themselves." — *V. Satir*

How many of us have heard, "Until I experienced the therapeutic relationship, I never felt heard by anyone in my life." Many people have said that about Milton Erickson. Feeling accepted is an essential part of healing. The beauty of the hypnotic relationship is that it can intensify this experience in a very short time. It is clear in this session that Joan feels this acceptance more and more as they move along.

On reading the introduction to the case, I focused on two things: her strengths and the traumatic learnings or imprints she had received as a child. One indication of her strengths is the fact that, after escaping into a marriage that became abusive, she got out of it within one year. Another is the fact that she has been drug-free "for years now." That she chose not to succumb to the fear that the hepatitis B that had killed her mother would also kill her, but rather reacted positively to her father's conversation with her, indicated that she would probably react to Lankton positively. Other resources to work with are that she is clear about what she feels, and she knows the feeling of self-confidence and being in control when she is at work.

Her loss of her mother, the emotional distance from her father, and the loss of her grandmother were traumatic events around which, I believe, she organized her image of herself and underlying assumptions about her relationships.

> "Reclaim the parts of the self that are
> outside of conscious control."
> — *Stephen Gilligan, Ph.D.*

Gilligan has said: "When someone wants something, I also entertain the complementarity—the other side of the coin. . .I support their holding on and letting go." It is what Satir calls the profound acceptance of *all* parts of the self.

In the initial parts of the session, Lankton guides Joan to access a strength—her sense of control in her job, absorbing and reframing her "falling apart," accepting it: "Are you already preparing to fall apart or do you wait...?" and reframing it: "Or how do you do that? When do you know when to start? Do you need like a special amount of shopping time ahead to know...?" Here he is beginning to give her control over it, using her "observing self," which is the beginning of enabling her to dissociate, to be "part of and apart from," and to think about what triggers this feeling. He then adds: "Only so many shopping days to get my falling apart together?" There is humor in this, and at this point, he has stood up and walked across the room to get a tissue, and he blows his nose. This is a pattern shift that can stimulate some kind of response in her. Physical movement *always* affects pattern change.

## Teaching and Role Modeling

Throughout the session, Lankton intersperses his own experiential learning to counteract the blanks or emotional myopia that came from Joan's own background. Earlier he focuses on her ability to separate and to stand up for herself. Here is an example of metaphoric modeling: "And there's sometimes when the world requires that. You know, when I get those phone calls when they want to sell me something I don't need...And you have to listen to them or, if you have to, say 'Look, don't call me up. I don't want to hear these phone calls'" (voice-tone change).

In reading this, I was reminded of the February man, in which, although Erickson structured it differently, a loving figure fills in lacunae of experience, creating out of the context of the hypnotic connection a bonding relationship in which childhood learnings can take place and be reorganized. Lankton shares with Joan the levels of his relationship with his children and with his own reactions, both positive and negative, all the self-questioning, failed expectations, tailored to her own self-doubts and struggles. In typical Ericksonian fashion, he uses a lot of coaching and generalizations until he gets to the human condition we are all in: "Grappling with the human condition is a lovely piece of cake." To this she replies, "Right." Then comes another reframe having to do with her self-esteem. It goes from "God, there is something wrong with me," to "God, the world is a little weird, but this is the human condition," to "The world needs not to disenfranchise people because they're not married, child-rearing consumers...and I feel the result of that and it kind of pisses me off, actually." She replies, "You are absolutely right." They now move from self-image to maturing (takes the fun out of things) to her toolbox.

"We forget how powerful our words are."
    —*Kay Thompson, D.D.S.*

The theme of the toolbox is a wonderful and reassuring metaphor for learning that Lankton uses throughout the session to anchor the conversational models with his own children, sharing with her a multilevel experience of kindness, compassion, geniality, and shared fun. Many words are repeated over and over: her ability to articulate, amazement, dignity, good feelings, loving mother, proud mother. Toward the end, there is an integration: "Mothering, daughtering, sharing, needing nurturing, and giggling. We started with words like 'yokel' and 'redneck,' we're looking up 'dignity' and. . . . "

## Creativity and Integration

Moshe Feldenkrais, the Israeli physicist and judo black belt who developed a unique system of hypnotic communication between mind and body, defined elegance as the exact amount of energy needed to fulfill the function—no more and no less.

Moving to imagery and age regression, Lankton speaks of "coming back up to a picture of the present of yourself. . . this time when you scan the pictures of your son, hold onto that good feeling. The more you relax, the more there is a capability of letting your imagination drive your feeling state. The more tense you are. . . the more your feeling state is stabilized by your body position." He anchors that good feeling of Joan by her holding her wrist as a signal to hold onto those feelings. He then takes her back to her pictures of herself as a little girl, holding onto her good feelings about herself. Her unconscious holds onto being a caring mother, while her conscious keeps picturing her three-year-old self. Then he flips it, and leads her to having a conversation between her child self and her loving mother self. There is an exchange between the mother who is "proud and amazed and sad and tender and happy and loving and caring" and the little girl "whose sadnesses and happinesses and joys. . . in the quest for the amazement that a little girl has." He later moves to an ideomotor signal, a feeling in her heart or stomach that tells her conscious mind that her unconscious is "having a need." He then moves her to her little-girl giggle and reframes the anxiety: "Let the giggle replace the vibration of anxiety. Ask her if it would be okay with her if you used her giggle to replace that sense of anxiety." He further dissociates her: "And then watch yourself watching her, if you can." Then, "Review that agreement we just made (mother and child) and make sure it fits your sense of dignity as a person and your values, and add anything to it you'd like to have."

Lankton deepens the trance and Joan talks with her mother about her "going away" and how "not understanding really hurts." She moves through layers and layers of feeling and association—coming upon "the process of mothering, daughtering, sharing, needing, nurturing, and giggling," weaving into the past, present, and future all that she had missed, and all that she can now create to give to her son and to herself.

Lankton's story of the boy who was saved by the spirit of his grandfather is another deep variation of the theme that runs throughout—that loss and separation can be associated with nurturing and protection and loving instead of abandonment and rejection. There is an elegant shape to this work that touches on this theme in every aspect of Joan's life and personality—and that touches us all.

Reading this evoked in my own mind and heart the artistry of Milton Erickson, and how it is possible for one human being to tap the exquisite creativity in the mind and the heart of another.

## References

Erickson, M. H., & Rossi, E. L. (1979). *Hypnotherapy: An exploratory casebook.* New York: Irvington.

Parsons-Fein, J. A. (1992). In August *Newsletter.* New York: The New York Milton H. Erickson Society for Psychotherapy and Hypnosis.

Rossi, E. L., Ed. (1980). *The collected papers of Milton H. Erickson, Volume IV.* New York: Irvington.